WORDS
THAT BURN

Also by Josephine Hart

Fiction

Damage
Sin
Oblivion
The Stillest Day
The Reconstructionist

Poetry Anthology

Catching Life by the Throat

WORDS THAT BURN

HOW TO READ POETRY AND WHY

POEMS FROM EIGHT GREAT POETS

JOSEPHINE HART

virago

VIRAGO

First published in Great Britain in 2008 by Virago Press

This compilation and introductory material
copyright © Josephine Hart 2008

The moral right of the author has been asserted.

Complimentary CD, recording copyright ℗ British Library.
Performances, in order of appearance, by: Charles Dance, Joanna David,
Greg Wise, Robert Hardy, Tom Hollander, Lindsay Duncan, Eileen Atkins,
Edward Fox, Dominic West, Elizabeth McGovern, Mark Strong, Emilia Fox,
Jeremy Irons, Felicity Kendal, Nancy Carroll and Alan Cox.

Photograph credits: Elizabeth Bishop © Bettmann/Corbis; Robert Browning by
George Frederic Watts © National Portrait Gallery, London; Lord Byron,
John Milton and Percy Bysshe Shelley © Mary Evans Picture Library; Robert Frost
© courtesy of Dartmouth College Library, Special Collections; Robert Lowell by
Alfred Eisenstadt/*Life* magazine © Time Inc.; Christina G. Rossetti © Lebrecht Images

Copyright Acknowledgements on pages 251–2 constitute
an extension of this copyright page.

A CIP catalogue record for this book is
available from the British Library.

ISBN 978-1-84408-554-5

Typeset in Goudy by M Rules
Printed and bound in Great Britain by
Clays Ltd, St Ives plc

Papers used by Virago are natural, renewable and recyclable
products made from wood grown in sustainable forests and certified
in accordance with the rules of the Forest Stewardship Council.

Mixed Sources
Product group from well-managed
forests and other controlled sources
www.fsc.org Cert no. SGS-COC-004081
© 1996 Forest Stewardship Council

Virago Press
An imprint of
Little, Brown Book Group
100 Victoria Embankment
London EC4Y 0DY

An Hachette Livre UK Company
www.hachettelivre.co.uk

www.virago.co.uk

In praise of actors and their mysterious art,
and of poets and their mystical power.

CONTENTS

WORDS
THAT BURN

ACKNOWLEDGEMENTS

I fall ever deeper into debt. The generosity with which I am granted further credit is little short of heroic. Alas, the words 'thank you' are the least adequate in the language. Yet I say them again: to the ever-lengthening cast of great actors who have read for me at the British Library and without whose unwavering commitment *The Josephine Hart Poetry Hour* would not take place – Dame Eileen Atkins, Claire Bloom, Bono, Tom Burke, Simon Callow, Nancy Carroll, Alan Cox, Brian Cox, Marton Csokas, Sinéad Cusack, Charles Dance, Hugh Dancy, Joanna David, Brian Dennehy, Lindsay Duncan, Ralph Fiennes, Peter Florence, Edward Fox, Emilia Fox, Bob Geldof, Alexander Gilmour, Julian Glover, Lord Gowrie (Grey), Rupert Graves, Robert Hardy, Tom Hollander, Jeremy Irons, Max Irons, Felicity Kendal, Damian Lewis, Helen McCrory, Ian McDiarmid, Elizabeth McGovern, Sir Roger Moore, Sir John Mortimer, Harold Pinter, Edna O'Brien, Charlotte Rampling, Kelly Reilly, Dan Stevens, Juliet Stevenson, Mark Strong, Harriet Walter, Dominic West and Greg Wise; to Lennie Goodings, my publisher at Virago Press, to whose dedication and publishing brilliance I owe this book and our 2006 collection, *Catching Life by the Throat* – for all of us the realisation of a dream – and to my editor Rowan Cope, who has with grace guided me to deadlines I was convinced were impossible; to Hachette Digital and Sarah Shrubb, who reassured a technophobe that we would indeed have a CD, and to Garrick Hagon of The Story Circle, who saw to it that we did; to Ed Victor, who remains, as ever, in all ways, 'the good shepherd' . . . he never falters and he knows the way home; to Grainne Fox of Ed Victor Ltd, for her unstinting encouragement and her discerning advice; to Angharad Wood of Tavistock Wood, whose deep insight and intelligence is matched only by her supreme organisational abilities, and to her assistant Olivia Bennett, who remained calm and efficient during the (for me) nightmare search for source notes (these notes resided in the many biographies and essays that I have plundered over the years, ever in awe of the deep learning of their authors, on whose research and erudition I am completely reliant; my errors are my own – I apologise in advance); to Bob Geldof for his passionate belief that the programmes should be broadcast, to Denys Blakeway, Madeleine Brolly and Jo Coombes of Blakeway Productions and to BBC Radio Four. Finally my deep gratitude to everyone at the British Library, and most especially to Jill Finney, Lara Jukes, Heather Norman-Soderlind, Jon Fawcett, the curators and the technical team, Sav Ioannau, Savan Modha, Gary Butler and Colin Day, and to Vivian Critelli of Leith's. Everyone since our first event has been consistently supportive and totally efficient.

My family, Maurice, Adam and Edward, loyally attend each of the readings; I gather that I go 'from strength to strength' . . . The loving lies continue.

Josephine Hart, 2008

INTRODUCTION

How do you possess a poem? Well, 'same as for love'. Pay attention to it. Listen to it. It will speak to you on the page. Silently. Or you may wish, as the critic Harold Bloom advises, to speak it out loud to yourself. In time, as he believes, you may come to feel that you have written it. The poet won't mind! Your interpretation 'may differ from the author's and be equally valid – it may even be better'. Eliot, giving us absolution. Poets came on earth 'to startle us out of our sleep-of-death into a more capacious sense of life'.

Decades have passed since I first embarked on this strange adventure of bringing to an audience great poetry read by our finest actors. And each time, at each new event, as I listen to some of the greatest language ever written, I am again transported. The fact that I am also on the stage to give my short introduction to the poet's life and work is irrelevant. The poetry sounds out and I 'trip . . . into the boundless', as Frost described it. It is a thrilling journey and is, I believe, the secret of what happens *underneath* at these readings. We endeavour to transmit to our audience what the critic Ben Yagoda called 'The Sound on the Page'. It is the sound of the human voice 'somehow entangled in the words and fastened to the page for the ear of the imagination'. Frost, again.

Within the imagination, suddenly, the poem finds *you*. You may not have been aware that you were searching for it. Indeed the poet himself or herself may have been responding to what Eliot (in discussing Gottfried Benn's lecture on the lyric) described as 'the something germinating in him for which he must find words'; and in finding language for 'the something' create the lines which we delight to '*overhear*'. When I first '*overheard*' 'Footfalls echo in the memory / Down the passage which we did not take / Towards the door we never opened / Into the rose-garden', the shock of recognition was physical.

1

I couldn't move. I was in a sense, mesmerised. Then the words seemed to take up residence, to settle down, so to speak, within me. As did the lines which follow: 'My words echo / Thus, in your mind. / But to what purpose / Disturbing the dust on a bowl of rose-leaves / I do not know.' I still don't. I remain, however, addicted to the echo, which continues to haunt and delight me.

By nature, I am an all or nothing girl, so line after line in poem after poem of T. S. Eliot's tumbled into my mind. In poetic terms I had found my man. He – thankfully – did not demand exclusivity. I love, with passion, others, many of whom are in this book. Robert Frost reminds us of the silken unbreakable thread between poetry and love. Each begins 'in delight and ends in wisdom'. Like love, which always desires possession, a poem can indeed become yours, for ever.

It was in that belief I started Gallery Poets, so called because the Odette Gilbert Gallery in Cork Street allowed us, with incredible generosity, to hold our readings there in the late 1980s. I really have no idea how I managed to persuade the brilliant actors who took part, including the late Sir Alan Bates, Robert Stephens and Gary Bond – 'Hello. You don't know me, but I'd love you to read . . .'. My generous victims also included Eileen Atkins, Edward Fox and Michael Gough, on whose talent and kindness I still ruthlessly prey, and with whom I developed an Eliot programme, *Let Us Go Then, You and I*, which we presented at the Lyric, Hammersmith. ('They queued and fought for tickets' – a review by Valerie Grove which continues to delight us.) The production eventually moved, for a month, then extended to six weeks, to the Lyric, Shaftesbury Avenue, the first and only time poetry has enjoyed a West End run. Michael Grandage has invited us to reprise that programme at the prestigious Donmar Warehouse – we are honoured. Since 2004, the British Library has provided us with what we hope is a permanent home. We are profoundly happy there, and profoundly grateful.

Sometimes we leave home for a visit. Last year, the National Library of Ireland invited us to read the poetry of W. B. Yeats. 'Delighted!' we replied. Bono, Sinéad Cusack and Jeremy Irons caught every nuance in poetry that has 'gathered up the heart's desire of the world'. It was, truly, a night to remember. This year on 7 April, at the invitation of the New York Public Library and to mark the American publication by Norton of *Catching Life by the Throat*, we presented the poetry of Robert Frost and Robert Lowell. The great American actor Brian Dennehy and our own brilliant Mark Strong read the work of these haunting poets with perfect poise and grace. We have been asked to return to that most beautiful library and we will, soon. We have donated to the library two hundred copies of the American edition of *Catching Life by the Throat*. On the accompanying CD, the poetry of W. H. Auden is read by Ralph Fiennes; Emily Dickinson by Juliet Stevenson; T. S. Eliot by Edward Fox, Ian McDiarmid and Helen McCrory; Rudyard Kipling by Roger Moore; Philip Larkin by Harold Pinter; Marianne Moore by Elizabeth McGovern; Sylvia Plath by Harriet Walter; and W. B. Yeats by Sinéad Cusack and Bob Geldof. The UK edition and CD published in 2006 were, thanks to the generosity and cooperation of their publishers Virago and Hachette Digital, of the British Library and all of the actors, sent free of charge to every secondary school in Britain. We plan to do the same with *Words That Burn*, the title of which is taken from Thomas Gray's lovely line, 'Thoughts, that breathe, and words, that burn'.

We hope that in the poems in this new collection you will find 'the very image of life expressed in eternal truth'. Certainly you will find the floating image of love, which is harder, much harder even for poets to catch. And that's the truth about love! Rossetti's 'When I am dead, my dearest / Sing no sad songs for me' sounds a gentler note than that of the woman's 'old-fashioned tirade— / loving, rapid, merciless', as it 'breaks like the Atlantic Ocean on my head' in 'Man and Wife', Lowell's savage poem of love and sex gone wrong. Nobody does it better. Browning, the mysterious, whose own life was a love-filled idyll with Elizabeth Barrett Browning, gives us in his sinister masterpiece 'My Last Duchess' a study in exquisitely calibrated moral brutality. However, the true poet of terror is Frost. Do not let his American country beat-simple speech deceive you. Byron, in his talking poetry (he wrote, he said, 'exactly as I talk') nails to the wall wickedly and wittily sexual duplicity both male and female in *Don Juan*. He also, in our excerpt from *Childe Harold's Pilgrimage*, measures out the cost of overweening ambition that makes the 'madmen who have made men mad'. (In the first decade of this century you may wish to name your own.) The child's cry of pain in Elizabeth Bishop's 'In the Waiting Room' is as penetrating as that of the woman in Munch's not-so-silent painting. Shelley, the incandescent, burning up everything around him, shaped out of personal devastation and at the age of only twenty-nine the inevitable *The Triumph of Life*: 'how Dante would have written had he written in English' according to Bloom, to whom 'poetry is the crown of imaginative literature . . . because it is a prophetic mode'. John Milton, whose *Paradise Lost* is a monument to awe-inspiring genius and sheer force of will, was born four hundred years ago. We have taken excerpts from Books I, IV and IX of *Paradise Lost*, in which we join Satan in the magnificence of his heroic defiance – 'What though the field be lost?' – and then follow him into the Garden of Eden, where, alas, he discovers Adam and Eve, and we discovered sin: It's an old story. Milton knew in 1667 what we know still: the mind remains 'its own place' and many would prefer, like Satan, 'to reign in Hell, than serve in Heav'n'. If the poetry of Dante is, in Shelley's phrase, 'a bridge thrown over time', Milton too continues to span the centuries.

Whatever the mysteries of poetry, it is 'ever accompanied by pleasure', as I hope you will find in this new collection and CD, on which the poetry of Elizabeth Bishop is read by Charles Dance; Robert Browning by Greg Wise and Robert Hardy; Lord Byron by Edward Fox, Eileen Atkins, Lindsay Duncan and Tom Hollander; Robert Frost and Robert Lowell by Mark Strong, Dominic West and Elizabeth McGovern; Milton by Emilia Fox, Jeremy Irons, Felicity Kendal and Greg Wise; Shelley by Alan Cox and Dominic West; and Christina Rossetti by Nancy Carroll and Joanna David. These actors, indeed all our actors, rehearse and read for no fee, no expenses. All monies over and above costs to the British Library go to the King George V Fund for Actors and Actresses.

If it is ever more difficult for me adequately to express my gratitude to them, it is impossible to express the absolute respect in which I hold them. Actors *never* tell you how hard they work – such reticence, alas, is not universal in the arts! In a conversation post-reading with Harold Pinter, we spoke of our dismay at the term 'luvvies', knowing, as he does even better than I, that while their art may be a form of alchemy – a gift from the gods as mysterious as that gifted to the poet – it is brought to fruition by dint of a discipline and a determination that would make a major-general glow with pride. In our much-lauded subsidised theatre much is donated by actors, many of whom with film and television work personally underwrite the cost of performing – six nights a week plus two matinees – and thus ensure that our great theatrical heritage is kept alive. I say thank you to them, and bravo!

ELIZABETH BISHOP

Elizabeth Bishop was born in Massachusetts in 1911. Her four short collections, *North and South* (1946), *A Cold Spring* (1955), *Questions of Travel* (1965) and *Geography III* (1976), won many literary awards including the National Book Critics Circle Award, the National Book Award and the Pulitzer Prize. She died in 1979.

ELIZABETH BISHOP

She came. She saw.
She changed the view.

'Everything has written under it – I have seen it.' Randall Jarrall is right. However, *what* Elizabeth Bishop saw was never quite what the rest of us see, nor indeed was it *how* we see it. And she knew it. She challenges us to look again. Her declared intention to combine 'the natural with the unnatural' gave us poetry as 'normal as sight . . . as artificial as a glass eye'. Well! It's hardly surprising that it takes us some time to adjust to the view. The landscape is unfamiliar. The temperature is arctic and is therefore less than seductive. However, deep treasure lies within the extreme geography of Elizabeth Bishop's 'ice writing'. She gifts us what few other poets ever have, a strange, exact hallucination of 'the always more successful surrealism of every-day life'. It is thus – after the necessary period of adjustment – that she becomes not just compelling but addictive. She is the poetic equiva-lent of a Dalí or de Chirico. Like them, she disturbs the universe and our limited perception of it. We are indeed 'far away within the view', longing to understand, if a little nervous of revelation. In 'Love Lies Sleeping' she word-paints, perhaps, inert terror in her portrait of the man . . . 'whose head has fallen over the edge of his bed, / whose face is turned / so that the image of / the city grows down into his open eyes / inverted and distorted. No. I mean / distorted and revealed, / if he sees it at all.' Is he, eyes wide open, in some hypnotised dream-state, a state she declared vital to the creation of her poetry? Is he dead? Miss Bishop herself is less than certain. She is the poet of question marks and when she answers it is rarely reassuring. 'I *think* [my italics] the man at the end is dead,' she told a rather startled Anne Stevenson. She'd been reading Newton's 'Optiks' during the writing of the poem – 'Reflections, Refractions . . . and Colours of Light' were as much her obsession as the subject of his masterpiece. (Is Bishop uniquely the only poet to have worked grinding binoculars at a US Navy shop?) Newton, whose work of discovery inspired eighteenth-century poets, is not normally a presiding figure in twentieth-century poetry. Nor indeed is Darwin, whose continued literary influence lies more within fiction. Bishop, the poet of vision, deeply admired his 'heroic obser-vations . . . his eyes fixed on facts and minute details, sinking or sliding giddily off into the unknown' and they became scientific inspiration to her own poetic discoveries. Though Elizabeth Bishop's four small collections, *North and South*, *A Cold Spring*, *Questions of Travel* and *Geography III*, would in time win many awards, includ-ing the National Book Award and the Pulitzer Prize, the first was, in 1940, firmly turned down by Random House, Viking and Simon and Schuster. It was finally published by Harcourt Brace in 1947. Originality comes at a price. James Merrill famously commented on her 'instinctive, modest, lifelong impersonation of an ordinary woman'. Perhaps she felt she needed the disguise. Her beginnings were traumatic. 'Although I think I have a prize "unhappy childhood" almost good enough for text-books – please don't think I dote on it.' She didn't. That does not mean she ever escaped it either. Her need for 'mastery', which Bonnie Costello sees as an 'urge for order and dominance confronting a volatile inner life,' is wholly understandable. She was born on 8 February 1911 in Worcester, Massachusetts, to William T. Bishop and Gertrude Bulmer [Boomer] Bishop. Her father died, aged thirty-nine, in October of that same year. Mother and child moved to Boston, and then to the charmingly named Great Village, Nova Scotia, in Canada, where Elizabeth's young life was, sadly, less than charmed. In 1916 when she was five, her mother, after a series of nervous breakdowns, was admitted to a state mental institution. Though Gertrude Bishop did not die until 1934, Elizabeth never saw her again. She was eventually returned to live with her mother's sister in Boston. Much was lost and far too early. In 'One Art' she notes that 'things seem filled with the intent / to be lost' and, with admirable, defiant courage, 'The art of losing isn't hard to master'. It wasn't easy either. Her adult life was one of often alcohol-fuelled departures, both emotional and geo-graphical. The poetry survived it all. She started writing at Vassar, the exclusive women's college in New York, where she befriended Mary McCarthy, whose novel *The Group* would profile her classmates. There remains considerable controversy as to whether the lesbian Lakey, played in the film by the ethereally beautiful Candice Bergen, was based on Bishop. Though Elizabeth Bishop had six intense, some-times concurrent, often tumultuous lesbian love affairs (one with Brazilian aristocrat Lota de Maceda Soares that lasted, on and off, for decades) love is not really her subject. Loss, deep-rooted in her personal history, and a subdued though multi-layered pattern of essential distancing, haunts her work. Her compulsive travelling inspires her poetic eloquence of elective rootlessness. But despite telling Randall Jarrall that 'Exile seems to work for me' she remained uncertain of its purpose. 'Is it lack of imagination that makes us come / to imagined places, not just stay at home? / Or could Pascal have been not entirely right / about just sitting quietly in one's room? . . . Should we have stayed at home, / wherever that may be?' From whichever perspective, in real or imagined landscapes, Bishop contains their discovery, and loss, within an ever-steely elegance of vision. 'I lost my mother's watch. And look! my last, or / next-to-last, of three loved houses went . . . I miss them, but it wasn't a disaster.' In truth the abyss was closer than she allowed. Though she was never, in the Lowell sense, a confessional poet (and profoundly disagreed with her old friend over what she saw as the cruel intimacy of 'Dolphin'), in her own later poems, particularly in her prize-winning collection *Geography III*, she returned – a poetic Livingstone – to the source. 'In the Waiting Room', itself a provoca-tive title, is a masterpiece of existential terror. As the seven-year-old Elizabeth sits quietly reading *National Geographic*: 'Suddenly, from inside, / came an *oh!* of pain / – Aunt Consuelo's voice– . . . What took

11

me / completely by surprise / was that it was *me*: / my voice, in my mouth . . . I knew that nothing stranger / had ever happened, that nothing / stranger could ever happen.' She was ill and in her sixty-sixth year when this poem was published. Baudelaire is right, 'genius is nothing more than childhood recovered at will'. Elizabeth Bishop, whose work Marianne Moore described as 'beautifully formulated aesthetic-moral mathematics', died in 1979 of a cerebral aneurysm. She asked that 'Awful, but cheerful' should be inscribed on her tombstone. Which changes the view. Again. The secondary characteristic of the glass eye is its incapacity for tears. Which leaves us with language – if we can find the words.

The Poems

She once said, 'we are driving to the interior'. One has been put on high alert. Perhaps, like 'The Gentleman of Shalott', we find the uncertainty exhilarating. After all, he 'loves that sense of constant re-adjustment'. Eliot, as C. K. Stead brilliantly observed, used his 'nerves' in 'Prufrock'. Bishop's is also an art of the nerves, in her case optic. 'Love Lies Sleeping' does not denote repose. As dawn comes we must 'clear away what presses on the brain' as 'the day-springs of the morning strike . . . alarms for the expected'. No going back to sleep, then.

Le Roy, in 'Songs for a Colored Singer', probably sleeps soundly. Though his woman wonders 'Le Roy, just how much are we owing? / Something I can't comprehend, / the more we got the more we spend.' An eternal mystery and not just in the Le Roy household. Well, 'life's like that', a line from 'The Moose' (twenty years to complete – 'revise, revise, revise', a trait noted by her friend, the arch-reviser himself, Lowell), and it is sometimes in opposition to Art, compelling us to choose. Would we, as she insists in 'The Imaginary Iceberg', 'rather have the iceberg than the ship, / although it meant the end of travel'? Art, like icebergs, which 'behoove the soul', is part-hidden, 'self-made from elements least visible', and is often dangerous to the ship of life, being as it is an obsession.

'Crusoe in England' knows obsession, knows it well and also knows its price. He remembers the moment: 'Just when I thought I couldn't stand it / another minute longer, Friday came.' Perfect. This blindingly brilliant poem was inspired by Darwin, about whose obsession Bishop wrote, 'What one seems to want in art, in experiencing it, is the same thing necessary for its creation, a self-forgetting, perfectly useless concentration.' Defoe was also self-forgetting, publishing his masterpiece as being that of an anonymous survivor of a shipwreck. He knew we'd find him out.

Bishop's Larkin-like genius for the sense of place – often most powerful in those who fear displacement – is again clear in 'Filling Station': 'Oh, but it is dirty!' Attention. 'Be careful with that match!' And in that line she's got us. Beyond the dirt and possible danger, she notes with heartbreaking accuracy, 'Somebody embroidered the doily.' And continues her enumeration of small graces in unexpected places: 'Somebody / arranges the rows of cans / so that they softly say: ESSO–SO–SO–SO / to high-strung automobiles.' She ends with an almost casual elegy: 'Somebody loves us all.'

'One Art' and 'In the Waiting Room' are late poems. They afford us no place to hide. 'Lose something every day . . . – Even losing you (the joking voice, a gesture / I love) I shan't have lied. It's evident / the art of losing's not too hard to master / though it may look like (*Write* it!) like disaster.' It's lines like that that make one, initially a reluctant convert, tremble. The congregation grows larger day by day; one notes in pews marked 'reserved' a Nobel Laureate, Heaney; a Poet Laureate, Motion; Fenton, winner of the Queen's Medal for Poetry. It's perfectly possible that Elizabeth Bishop, who avoided myth and grand statements but who found 'In the Waiting Room' one of literature's most frightening, and frightened, voices – that of the terrified child – is one of the greatest poets of the twentieth century. And that is perhaps what frightens us: in our own blindness we might have missed her.

The Gentleman of Shalott

Which eye's his eye?
Which limb lies
next the mirror?
For neither is clearer
nor a different color
than the other,
nor meets a stranger
in this arrangement
of leg and leg and
arm and so on.
To his mind
it's the indication
of a mirrored reflection
somewhere along the line
of what we call the spine.

He felt in modesty
his person was
half looking-glass,
for why should he
be doubled?
The glass must stretch
down his middle,
or rather down the edge.
But he's in doubt
as to which side's in or out
of the mirror.
There's little margin for error,

but there's no proof, either.
And if half his head's reflected,
thought, he thinks, might be affected.

But he's resigned
to such economical design.
If the glass slips
he's in a fix—
only one leg, etc. But
while it stays put
he can walk and run
and his hands can clasp one
another. The uncertainty
he says he
finds exhilarating. He loves
that sense of constant re-adjustment.
He wishes to be quoted as saying at present:
'Half is enough.'

Love Lies Sleeping

Earliest morning, switching all the tracks
that cross the sky from cinder star to star,
    coupling the ends of streets
    to trains of light,

now draw us into daylight in our beds;
and clear away what presses on the brain:
    put out the neon shapes
    that float and swell and glare

down the gray avenue between the eyes
in pinks and yellows, letters and twitching signs.
    Hang-over moons, wane, wane!
    From the window I see

an immense city, carefully revealed,
made delicate by over-workmanship,
    detail upon detail,
    cornice upon façade,

reaching so languidly up into
a weak white sky, it seems to waver there.
    (Where it has slowly grown
    in skies of water-glass

from fused beads of iron and copper crystals,
the little chemical 'garden' in a jar
    trembles and stands again,
    pale blue, blue-green, and brick.)

The sparrows hurriedly begin their play.
Then, in the West, 'Boom!' and a cloud of smoke.
   'Boom!' and the exploding ball
   of blossom blooms again.

(And all the employees who work in plants
where such a sound says 'Danger,' or once said 'Death,'
   turn in their sleep and feel
   the short hairs bristling

on backs of necks.) The cloud of smoke moves off.
A shirt is taken off a threadlike clothes-line.
   Along the street below
   the water-wagon comes

throwing its hissing, snowy fan across
peelings and newspapers. The water dries
   light-dry, dark-wet, the pattern
   of the cool watermelon.

I hear the day-springs of the morning strike
from stony walls and halls and iron beds,
   scattered or grouped cascades,
   alarms for the expected:

queer cupids of all persons getting up,
whose evening meal they will prepare all day,
   you will dine well
   on his heart, on his, and his,

so send them about your business affectionately,
dragging in the streets their unique loves.
   Scourge them with roses only,
   be light as helium,

for always to one, or several, morning comes,
whose head has fallen over the edge of his bed,
    whose face is turned
    so that the image of

the city grows down into his open eyes
inverted and distorted. No. I mean
    distorted and revealed,
    if he sees it at all.

Crusoe in England

A new volcano has erupted,
the papers say, and last week I was reading
where some ship saw an island being born:
at first a breath of steam, ten miles away;
and then a black fleck—basalt, probably—
rose in the mate's binoculars
and caught on the horizon like a fly.
They named it. But my poor old island's still
un-rediscovered, un-renamable.
None of the books has ever got it right.

Well, I had fifty-two
miserable, small volcanoes I could climb
with a few slithery strides—
volcanoes dead as ash heaps.
I used to sit on the edge of the highest one
and count the others standing up,
naked and leaden, with their heads blown off.
I'd think that if they were the size
I thought volcanoes should be, then I had
become a giant;
and if I had become a giant,
I couldn't bear to think what size
the goats and turtles were,
or the gulls, or the overlapping rollers
—a glittering hexagon of rollers
closing and closing in, but never quite,
glittering and glittering, though the sky
was mostly overcast.

My island seemed to be
a sort of cloud-dump. All the hemisphere's
left-over clouds arrived and hung
above the craters—their parched throats
were hot to touch.

Was that why it rained so much?
And why sometimes the whole place hissed?
The turtles lumbered by, high-domed,
hissing like teakettles.
(And I'd have given years, or taken a few,
for any sort of kettle, of course.)
The folds of lava, running out to sea,
would hiss. I'd turn. And then they'd prove
to be more turtles.
The beaches were all lava, variegated,
black, red, and white, and gray;
the marbled colors made a fine display.
And I had waterspouts. Oh,
half a dozen at a time, far out,
they'd come and go, advancing and retreating,
their heads in cloud, their feet in moving patches
of scuffed-up white.
Glass chimneys, flexible, attenuated,
sacerdotal beings of glass . . . I watched
the water spiral up in them like smoke.
Beautiful, yes, but not much company.

I often gave way to self-pity.
'Do I deserve this? I suppose I must.
I wouldn't be here otherwise. Was there
a moment when I actually chose this?
I don't remember, but there could have been.'
What's wrong about self-pity, anyway?
With my legs dangling down familiarly

over a crater's edge, I told myself
'Pity should begin at home.' So the more
pity I felt, the more I felt at home.

The sun set in the sea; the same odd sun
rose from the sea,
and there was one of it and one of me.
The island had one kind of everything:
one tree snail, a bright violet-blue
with a thin shell, crept over everything,
over the one variety of tree,

a sooty, scrub affair.
Snail shells lay under these in drifts
and, at a distance,
you'd swear that they were beds of irises.
There was one kind of berry, a dark red.
I tried it, one by one, and hours apart.
Sub-acid, and not bad, no ill effects;
and so I made home-brew. I'd drink
the awful, fizzy, stinging stuff
that went straight to my head
and play my home-made flute
(I think it had the weirdest scale on earth)
and, dizzy, whoop and dance among the goats.
Home-made, home-made! But aren't we all?
I felt a deep affection for
the smallest of my island industries.
No, not exactly, since the smallest was
a miserable philosophy.

Because I didn't know enough.
Why didn't I know enough of something?
Greek drama or astronomy? The books
I'd read were full of blanks;

the poems—well, I tried
reciting to my iris-beds,
'They flash upon that inward eye,
which is the bliss . . .' The bliss of what?
One of the first things that I did
when I got back was look it up.

The island smelled of goat and guano.
The goats were white, so were the gulls,
and both too tame, or else they thought
I was a goat, too, or a gull.
Baa, baa, baa and *shriek, shriek, shriek,*
baa . . . shriek . . . baa . . . I still can't shake
them from my ears; they're hurting now.
The questioning shrieks, the equivocal replies
over a ground of hissing rain
and hissing, ambulating turtles
got on my nerves.

When all the gulls flew up at once, they sounded
like a big tree in a strong wind, its leaves.
I'd shut my eyes and think about a tree,
an oak, say, with real shade, somewhere.
I'd heard of cattle getting island-sick.
I thought the goats were.
One billy-goat would stand on the volcano
I'd christened *Mont d'Espoir* or *Mount Despair*
(I'd time enough to play with names),
and bleat and bleat, and sniff the air.
I'd grab his beard and look at him.
His pupils, horizontal, narrowed up
and expressed nothing, or a little malice.
I got so tired of the very colors!
One day I dyed a baby goat bright red
with my red berries, just to see

something a little different.
And then his mother wouldn't recognize him.

Dreams were the worst. Of course I dreamed of food
and love, but they were pleasant rather
than otherwise. But then I'd dream of things
like slitting a baby's throat, mistaking it
for a baby goat. I'd have
nightmares of other islands
stretching away from mine, infinities
of islands, islands spawning islands,
like frogs' eggs turning into polliwogs
of islands, knowing that I had to live
on each and every one, eventually,
for ages, registering their flora,
their fauna, their geography.

Just when I thought I couldn't stand it
another minute longer, Friday came.
(Accounts of that have everything all wrong.)
Friday was nice.
Friday was nice, and we were friends.
If only he had been a woman!
I wanted to propagate my kind,
and so did he, I think, poor boy.
He'd pet the baby goats sometimes,
and race with them, or carry one around.
—Pretty to watch; he had a pretty body.

And then one day they came and took us off.

Now I live here, another island,
that doesn't seem like one, but who decides?
My blood was full of them; my brain
bred islands. But that archipelago

has petered out. I'm old.
I'm bored, too, drinking my real tea,
surrounded by uninteresting lumber.
The knife there on the shelf –
it reeked of meaning, like a crucifix.
It lived. How many years did I
beg it, implore it, not to break?
I knew each nick and scratch by heart,
the bluish blade, the broken tip,
the lines of wood-grain on the handle . . .
Now it won't look at me at all.
The living soul has dribbled away.
My eyes rest on it and pass on.

The local museum's asked me to
leave everything to them:
the flute, the knife, the shrivelled shoes,
my shedding goatskin trousers
(moths have got in the fur),
the parasol that took me such a time
remembering the way the ribs should go.
It still will work but, folded up,
looks like a plucked and skinny fowl.
How can anyone want such things?
—And Friday, my dear Friday, died of measles
seventeen years ago come March.

Songs for a Colored Singer

I
A washing hangs upon the line,
    but it's not mine.
None of the things that I can see
    belong to me.
The neighbors got a radio with an aerial;
    we got a little portable.
They got a lot of closet space;
    we got a suitcase.

I say, 'Le Roy, just how much are we owing?
Something I can't comprehend,
the more we got the more we spend . . .'
He only answers, 'Let's get going.'
Le Roy, you're earning too much money now.

I sit and look at our backyard
    and find it very hard.
What have we got for all his dollars and cents?
    —A pile of bottles by the fence.
He's faithful and he's kind
    but he sure has an inquiring mind.
He's seen a lot; he's bound to see the rest,
    and if I protest

Le Roy answers with a frown,
'Darling, when I earns I spends.
The world is wide; it still extends . . .

I'm going to get a job in the next town.'
Le Roy, you're earning too much money now.

II
The time has come to call a halt;
    and so it ends.
      He's gone off with his other friends.
      He needn't try to make amends,
this occasion's all his fault.
      Through rain and dark I see his face
      across the street at Flossie's place.
      He's drinking in the warm pink glow
      to th' accompaniment of the piccolo.*

The time has come to call a halt.
I met him walking with Varella
and hit him twice with my umbrella.
Perhaps that occasion was my fault,
but the time has come to call a halt.

Go drink your wine and go get tight.
    Let the piccolo play.
      I'm sick of all your fussing anyway.
      Now I'm pursuing my own way.
I'm leaving on the bus tonight.
      Far down the highway wet and black
      I'll ride and ride and not come back.
      I'm going to go and take the bus
      and find someone monogamous.

*Jukebox

ELIZABETH BISHOP

The time has come to call a halt.
I've borrowed fifteen dollars fare
and it will take me anywhere.
For this occasion's all his fault.
The time has come to call a halt.

One Art

The art of losing isn't hard to master;
so many things seem filled with the intent
to be lost that their loss is no disaster.

Lose something every day. Accept the fluster
of lost door keys, the hour badly spent.
The art of losing isn't hard to master.

Then practice losing farther, losing faster:
places, and names, and where it was you meant
to travel. None of these will bring disaster.

I lost my mother's watch. And look! my last, or
next-to-last, of three loved houses went.
The art of losing isn't hard to master.

I lost two cities, lovely ones. And, vaster,
some realms I owned, two rivers, a continent.
I miss them, but it wasn't a disaster.

—Even losing you (the joking voice, a gesture
I love) I shan't have lied. It's evident
the art of losing's not too hard to master
though it may look like (*Write* it!) like disaster.

The Imaginary Iceberg

We'd rather have the iceberg than the ship,
although it meant the end of travel.
Although it stood stock-still like cloudy rock
and all the sea were moving marble.
We'd rather have the iceberg than the ship;
we'd rather own this breathing plain of snow
though the ship's sails were laid upon the sea
as the snow lies undissolved upon the water.
O solemn, floating field,
are you aware an iceberg takes repose
with you, and when it wakes may pasture on your snows?

This is a scene a sailor'd give his eyes for.
The ship's ignored. The iceberg rises
and sinks again; its glassy pinnacles
correct elliptics in the sky.
This is a scene where he who treads the boards
is artlessly rhetorical. The curtain
is light enough to rise on finest ropes
that airy twists of snow provide.
The wits of these white peaks
spar with the sun. Its weight the iceberg dares
upon a shifting stage and stands and stares.

This iceberg cuts its facets from within.
Like jewelry from a grave
it saves itself perpetually and adorns
only itself, perhaps the snows

which so surprise us lying on the sea.
Good-bye, we say, good-bye, the ship steers off
where waves give in to one another's waves
and clouds run in a warmer sky.
Icebergs behoove the soul
(both being self-made from elements least visible)
to see them so: fleshed, fair, erected indivisible.

Filling Station

Oh, but it is dirty!
—this little filling station,
oil-soaked, oil-permeated
to a disturbing, over-all
black translucency.
Be careful with that match!

Father wears a dirty,
oil-soaked monkey suit
that cuts him under the arms,
and several quick and saucy
and greasy sons assist him
(it's a family filling station),
all quite thoroughly dirty.

Do they live in the station?
It has a cement porch
behind the pumps, and on it
a set of crushed and grease-
impregnated wickerwork;
on the wicker sofa
a dirty dog, quite comfy.

Some comic books provide
the only note of color—
of certain color. They lie
upon a big dim doily
draping a taboret

(part of the set),
beside a big hirsute begonia.

Why the extraneous plant?
Why the taboret?
Why, oh why, the doily?
(Embroidered in daisy stitch
with marguerites, I think,
and heavy with gray crochet.)

Somebody embroidered the doily.
Somebody waters the plant,
or oils it, maybe. Somebody
arranges the rows of cans
so that they softly say:
ESSO—SO—SO—SO
to high-strung automobiles.
Somebody loves us all.

In the Waiting Room

In Worcester, Massachusetts,
I went with Aunt Consuelo
to keep her dentist's appointment
and sat and waited for her
in the dentist's waiting room.
It was winter. It got dark
early. The waiting room
was full of grown-up people,
arctics and overcoats,
lamps and magazines.
My aunt was inside
what seemed like a long time
and while I waited I read
the *National Geographic*
(I could read) and carefully
studied the photographs:
the inside of a volcano,
black, and full of ashes;
then it was spilling over
in rivulets of fire.
Osa and Martin Johnson
dressed in riding breeches,
laced boots, and pith helmets.
A dead man slung on a pole
—'Long Pig,' the caption said.
Babies with pointed heads
wound round and round with string;
black, naked women with necks

wound round and round with wire
like the necks of light bulbs.
Their breasts were horrifying.
I read it right straight through.
I was too shy to stop.
And then I looked at the cover:
the yellow margins, the date.

Suddenly, from inside,
came an *oh!* of pain
—Aunt Consuelo's voice—
not very loud or long.
I wasn't at all surprised;
even then I knew she was
a foolish, timid woman.
I might have been embarrassed,
but wasn't. What took me
completely by surprise
was that it was *me*:
my voice, in my mouth.
Without thinking at all
I was my foolish aunt,
I—we—were falling, falling,
our eyes glued to the cover
of the *National Geographic*,
February, 1918.

I said to myself: three days
and you'll be seven years old.
I was saying it to stop
the sensation of falling off
the round, turning world
into cold, blue-black space.
But I felt: you are an *I*,
you are an *Elizabeth*,

you are one of *them*.
Why should *you* be one, too?
I scarcely dared to look
to see what it was I was.
I gave a sidelong glance
—I couldn't look any higher—
at shadowy gray knees,
trousers and skirts and boots
and different pairs of hands
lying under the lamps.
I knew that nothing stranger
had ever happened, that nothing
stranger could ever happen.

Why should I be my aunt,
or me, or anyone?
What similarities—
boots, hands, the family voice
I felt in my throat, or even
the *National Geographic*
and those awful hanging breasts—
held us all together
or made us all just one?
How—I didn't know any
word for it—how 'unlikely' . . .
How had I come to be here,
like them, and overhear
a cry of pain that could have
got loud and worse but hadn't?

The waiting room was bright
and too hot. It was sliding
beneath a big black wave,
another, and another.

Then I was back in it.
The War was on. Outside,
in Worcester, Massachusetts,
were night and slush and cold,
and it was still the fifth
of February, 1918.

ROBERT BROWNING

Robert Browning was born in London in 1812. He achieved
fame late in life with *The Ring and the Book* (1868/69). His
earlier works – *Dramatic Lyrics* (1842), *Men and Women*
(1855) and *Dramatis Personae* (1864) – testify to his
mastery of the dramatic monologue; many of the poems
are recognised as enduring works of genius. He was
married to the poet Elizabeth Barrett Browning.
He died in 1889.

ROBERT BROWNING

The Company He Kept...

'Within his work lies the mystery which belongs to the complex and within his life the much greater mystery which belongs to the simple.' G. K. Chesterton, his biographer.

Henry James, who noted everything, noted the essential doubleness in Browning. There are, he said, 'two Brownings – an esoteric and an exoteric. The former never peeps out in society, and the latter has not a suggestion of *Men and Women*.' 'The esoteric' sought his own company. Characters who lived 'on the dangerous edge of things. / The honest thief, the tender murderer, / The superstitious atheist'. They echo Nietzsche's 'pale criminal' and prefigure Freud's criminal 'from a sense of guilt – the utilisation of a deed in order to rationalise this feeling'. His characters, his Dramatis Personae, his Men and Women speak out to us in all their moral complexity in some of the greatest monologues in English literature: 'My Last Duchess', 'Porphyria's Lover', 'Bishop Blougram's Apology', 'Fra Lippo Lippi' ('You understand me: I'm a beast, I know"), 'Rabbi Ben Ezra', 'Karshish', 'Andrea del Sarto'. Their souls are revealed, unvarnished. 'Little else,' he said, 'was worth study.' Oscar Wilde said of Robert Browning (who would also write glorious love poetry and the ultimate hymn to nature, *Pippa Passes*: 'God's in his heaven – All's right with the world') that 'considered from a point of view of creator of character [Browning] ranks next to him who made Hamlet'.

He was born in Camberwell, London, into a harmonious and intellectual household on 7 May 1812 (the same year as Dickens: they are, according to Harold Bloom, the two great masters of the grotesque) to Sarah Anna Browning and Robert Browning Snr, a banker in the Bank of England, himself an aspiring poet with a passionate love of books, avidly collecting first editions.

Browning was educated mostly at home, learning music, languages, science, and – *mens sana in corpore sano* – boxing, fencing and riding, while, crucially, devouring everything in his father's magnificent library. This habit of intensive reading 'while it gave him knowledge of everything else left him in ignorance of the ignorance of the world', in Chesterton's telling phrase. In his early teenage years Shelley became an obsession and though he would later attempt to erase his manic scribbles in the margins of his treasured copy, he would also recall 'the passionate impatient struggles of a boy towards truth and love . . . growing pains accompanied by temporary distortion of the soul also', which his initial reading of *Queen Mab* inspired. There was nothing temporary about Browning's decision, aged eighteen, to become a poet and nothing else. His parents supported him in what must have been a less than reassuring career choice, however noble the vocation of poet would have seemed to Browning's father, whom Edmund Gosse believed saw in his son the realisation of his own thwarted ambition. There was a small allowance, Browning had 'the singular courage to decline to be rich' (though he would later change his mind!). These things are relative. 'My whole scheme of life,' Browning wrote, 'with its wants – material wants at least – was closely cut down and long ago calculated . . . So for my own future way in the world I have always refused to care . . .' That took self-belief. He needed it. Success came slowly, very slowly. In 1832, aged twenty, he published *Pauline*. Ten thousand words, some excellent reviews – but many were hostile, and alas, not a single copy was sold. Three years later 'Paracelsus' (1835) brought him favourable attention from Carlyle and Wordsworth, and a comparison (from Fox) with Shelley. However it was not a major success. Ten years later he would recall those who 'laughed my Paracelsus to scorn'. Worse was to come. 'Sordello', published in 1840, took him seven years to write and though it became a cult text for the Pre-Raphaelites it was savaged by the critics. He was almost thirty and almost finished. Two years later in 1842 *Dramatic Lyrics*, which includes some of his best work, went largely unnoticed. He continued to write, but he would be middle-aged before he achieved the success he deserved, with the publication of *The Ring and the Book*. This success came shortly after the death of his wife, one of England's most revered poets, Elizabeth Barrett Browning. He was married to her for sixteen years. Her star shone so high in the firmament that when Wordsworth died her name was canvassed as Poet Laureate, while his was not mentioned, 'even satirically'. 'I love your verses with all my heart', he wrote to her in January 1845, months after she'd published *Poems 1844* to enormous critical acclaim. She read on and halfway down the second page she read the astonishing declaration 'and I love you too'. Their story is well known: 547 letters, then secret meetings which finally led to an elopement and then flight to Italy. His invalided wife defied her deeply strange and controlling father to take her chances (which would include late motherhood) with the love of her life. 'Determined, dared, and done', one of his favourite lines from an eighteenth-century poem (Christopher Smart's 'A Song to David'), and which is quoted in a more sinister context in *The Ring and the Book*, applied to her as much as to him. The love poems did not come into being as mysteriously as the dramatic monologues did. They were open celebrations of their deep love and in his case this love came from an uncommonly capacious heart. He never resented her glory. *Men and Women* is dedicated to her with the words 'Here they are – my fifty men and women / Take them, Love / the book and me together: / Where the heart lies, let the brain lie also'. In 'Love Among the Ruins' he sets the whole panoply of heroic endeavour and monuments to ambition beside the human joy of an arranged meeting with the love of one's life and declares 'Love is best'. He meant it.

After Elizabeth's death Robert Browning's output continued to be prodigious and, at last, he was revered. 'Do you object to all this adulation?' he was asked once when surrounded by admirers. 'Object to it? I've waited forty years for it!' He died in 1889 aged seventy-seven from a heart condition, appropriately shortly after his son read out a telegram from his publisher to say that 'Asolando' had received excellent reviews. He was satisfied. He was buried at Westminster Abbey, an occasion of which Henry James wrote, 'A good many oddities and a good many great writers have been entombed in the Abbey but none of the odd ones have been so great and none of the great ones have been so odd.'

The Poems

He was, said Chesterton, 'the poet of desire'. John Bayley agrees. Indeed, Bayley believes that even Proust, had he come across it, would have been 'enchanted . . . by the astonishing concentration of desire' in Browning's 'Meeting at Night'. The 'desire' in that poem resolves itself delightfully in Blakeian satisfaction. However, as Browning knew, desire can be perverted. He understood 'the Corruption of Man's Heart'. In his sinister masterpiece 'My Last Duchess' and in 'Porphyria's Lover', each narrator is a cold-blooded murderer. The cliché cold-blooded understates the case. They are icy in their cruelty. They are unforgettable.

The poet, according to C. Day Lewis, 'listens in to his universe'. Another memorable voice in Browning's auditory universe is that of Andrea del Sarto – 'the Faultless Painter'. His 'Madonna of the Harpies' hangs in the Uffizi Gallery in Florence, in a room dedicated to his work. As Browning ponders in this monologue whether fault-lessness is in itself a fault in art he muses also on the price of love. Love, Vasari implies in *Lives of the Painters*, cost del Sarto his position at the French court. Del Sarto, on receipt of a letter from his wife Lucrezia, speedily left the court. Did she hint at infidelity? Hers? We do not know. Neither do we know who the 'cousin' is who waits for her, as del Sarto paints. The tension between love and art is examined by Browning in this wondrous masterpiece, a subtle web of questions to which the answers may be dangerous.

'The Lost Leader' is not subtle. Browning came to regret the feroc-ity of his condemnation of political betrayal, in this case of Wordsworth, who'd abandoned the Liberal cause. However, as a poem of disillu-sionment with a hero, it is lacerating. 'Just for a handful of silver he left us / Just for a riband to stick in his coat.' 'The Patriot', with its equally memorable opening line, 'It was roses, roses, all the way', tells of the savage reversal of fortune which can change today's hero into the criminal on his way to the gallows. It's an old story and an old warning. 'Memorabilia' catches beautifully the poet's delight as he looks in wonderment at the man who may once have seen 'Shelley plain'. Heroism, this time of the horse (Browning was an animal lover and a member of the Anti-Vivisection Society), triumphs in the galloping '"How They Brought the Good News from Ghent to Aix"', its technically dazzling rhythms reminiscent of Auden's 'Night Train'. Browning once wrote, 'Grow old along with me! / The best is yet to be.' His beloved Elizabeth did not grow old with him. However in one of his last poems, 'Prospice', he challenges death and proclaims, 'For sudden the worst turns the best to the brave . . . Then a light, then thy breast, / O thou soul of my soul! I shall clasp thee again, / And with God be the rest!' One hopes.

Porphyria's Lover

The rain set early in tonight,
    The sullen wind was soon awake,
It tore the elm-tops down for spite,
    And did its worst to vex the lake:
    I listened with heart fit to break.
When glided in Porphyria; straight
    She shut the cold out and the storm,
And kneeled and made the cheerless grate
    Blaze up, and all the cottage warm;
    Which done, she rose, and from her form
Withdrew the dripping cloak and shawl,
    And laid her soiled gloves by, untied
Her hat and let the damp hair fall,
    And, last, she sat down by my side
    And called me. When no voice replied,
She put my arm about her waist,
    And made her smooth white shoulder bare,
And all her yellow hair displaced,
    And, stooping, made my cheek lie there,
    And spread, o'er all, her yellow hair,
Murmuring how she loved me – she
    Too weak, for all her heart's endeavour,
To set its struggling passion free
    From pride, and vainer ties dissever,
    And give herself to me for ever.
But passion sometimes would prevail,
    Nor could tonight's gay feast restrain
A sudden thought of one so pale

For love of her, and all in vain:
  So, she was come through wind and rain.
Be sure I looked up at her eyes
  Happy and proud; at last I knew
Porphyria worshipped me; surprise
  Made my heart swell, and still it grew
  While I debated what to do.
That moment she was mine, mine, fair,
  Perfectly pure and good: I found
A thing to do, and all her hair
  In one long yellow string I wound
  Three times her little throat around,
And strangled her. No pain felt she;
  I am quite sure she felt no pain.
As a shut bud that holds a bee,
  I warily oped her lids: again
  Laughed the blue eyes without a stain.
And I untightened next the tress
  About her neck; her cheek once more
Blushed bright beneath my burning kiss:
  I propped her head up as before,
  Only, this time my shoulder bore
Her head, which droops upon it still:
  The smiling rosy little head,
So glad it has its utmost will,
  That all it scorned at once is fled,
  And I, its love, am gained instead!
Porphyria's love: she guessed not how
  Her darling one wish would be heard.
And thus we sit together now,
  And all night long we have not stirred,
  And yet God has not said a word!

My Last Duchess

Ferrara

That's my last Duchess painted on the wall,
Looking as if she were alive. I call
That piece a wonder, now: Frà Pandolf's hands
Worked busily a day, and there she stands.
Will't please you sit and look at her? I said
'Frà Pandolf' by design, for never read
Strangers like you that pictured countenance,
The depth and passion of its earnest glance,
But to myself they turned (since none puts by
The curtain I have drawn for you, but I)
And seemed as they would ask me, if they durst,
How such a glance came there; so, not the first
Are you to turn and ask thus. Sir, 'twas not
Her husband's presence only, called that spot
Of joy into the Duchess' cheek: perhaps
Frà Pandolf chanced to say 'Her mantle laps
Over my lady's wrist too much,' or 'Paint
Must never hope to reproduce the faint
Half-flush that dies along her throat': such stuff
Was courtesy, she thought, and cause enough
For calling up that spot of joy. She had
A heart – how shall I say? – too soon made glad,
Too easily impressed; she liked whate'er
She looked on, and her looks went everywhere.
Sir, 'twas all one! My favour at her breast,
The dropping of the daylight in the West,
The bough of cherries some officious fool

Broke in the orchard for her, the white mule
She rode with round the terrace – all and each
Would draw from her alike the approving speech,
Or blush, at least. She thanked men, – good! but thanked
Somehow – I know not how – as if she ranked
My gift of a nine-hundred-years-old name
With anybody's gift. Who'd stoop to blame
This sort of trifling? Even had you skill
In speech – (which I have not) – to make your will
Quite clear to such an one, and say, 'Just this
Or that in you disgusts me; here you miss,
Or there exceed the mark' – and if she let
Herself be lessoned so, nor plainly set
Her wits to yours, forsooth, and made excuse,
– E'en then would be some stooping; and I choose
Never to stoop. Oh sir, she smiled, no doubt,
Whene'er I passed her; but who passed without
Much the same smile? This grew; I gave commands;
Then all smiles stopped together. There she stands
As if alive. Will't please you rise? We'll meet
The company below, then. I repeat,
The Count your master's known munificence
Is ample warrant that no just pretence
Of mine for dowry will be disallowed;
Though his fair daughter's self, as I avowed
At starting, is my object. Nay, we'll go
Together down, sir. Notice Neptune, though,
Taming a sea-horse, thought a rarity,
Which Claus of Innsbruck cast in bronze for me!

Andrea del Sarto

(Called 'The Faultless Painter')

But do not let us quarrel any more,
No, my Lucrezia; bear with me for once:
Sit down and all shall happen as you wish.
You turn your face, but does it bring your heart?
I'll work then for your friend's friend, never fear,
Treat his own subject after his own way,
Fix his own time, accept too his own price,
And shut the money into this small hand
When next it takes mine. Will it? tenderly?
Oh, I'll content him, – but tomorrow, Love!
I often am much wearier than you think,
This evening more than usual, and it seems
As if – forgive now – should you let me sit
Here by the window with your hand in mine
And look a half-hour forth on Fiesole,
Both of one mind, as married people use,
Quietly, quietly the evening through,
I might get up tomorrow to my work
Cheerful and fresh as ever. Let us try.
Tomorrow, how you shall be glad for this!
Your soft hand is a woman of itself,
And mine the man's bared breast she curls inside.
Don't count the time lost, neither; you must serve
For each of the five pictures we require:
It saves a model. So! keep looking so –
My serpentining beauty, rounds on rounds!
– How could you ever prick those perfect ears,

Even to put the pearl there! oh, so sweet –
My face, my moon, my everybody's moon,
Which everybody looks on and calls his,
And, I suppose, is looked on by in turn,
While she looks – no one's: very dear, no less.
You smile? why, there's my picture ready made,
There's what we painters call our harmony!
A common greyness silvers everything, –
All in a twilight, you and I alike
– You, at the point of your first pride in me
(That's gone you know), – but I, at every point;
My youth, my hope, my art, being all toned down
To yonder sober pleasant Fiesole.
There's the bell clinking from the chapel-top;
That length of convent-wall across the way
Holds the trees safer, huddled more inside;
The last monk leaves the garden; days decrease,
And autumn grows, autumn in everything.
Eh? the whole seems to fall into a shape
As if I saw alike my work and self
And all that I was born to be and do,
A twilight-piece. Love, we are in God's hand.
How strange now, looks the life he makes us lead;
So free we seem, so fettered fast we are!
I feel he laid the fetter: let it lie!
This chamber for example – turn your head –
All that's behind us! You don't understand
Nor care to understand about my art,
But you can hear at least when people speak:
And that cartoon, the second from the door
– It is the thing, Love! so such things should be –
Behold Madonna! – I am bold to say.
I can do with my pencil what I know,
What I see, what at bottom of my heart
I wish for, if I ever wish so deep –

Do easily, too – when I say, perfectly,
I do not boast, perhaps: yourself are judge,
Who listened to the Legate's talk last week,
And just as much they used to say in France.
At any rate 'tis easy, all of it!
No sketches first, no studies, that's long past:
I do what many dream of, all their lives,
– Dream? strive to do, and agonize to do,
And fail in doing. I could count twenty such
On twice your fingers, and not leave this town,
Who strive – you don't know how the others strive
To paint a little thing like that you smeared
Carelessly passing with your robes afloat, –
Yet do much less, so much less, Someone says,
(I know his name, no matter) – so much less!
Well, less is more, Lucrezia: I am judged.
There burns a truer light of God in them,
In their vexed beating stuffed and stopped-up brain,
Heart, or whate'er else, than goes on to prompt
This low-pulsed forthright craftsman's hand of mine.
Their works drop groundward, but themselves, I know,
Reach many a time a heaven that's shut to me,
Enter and take their place there sure enough,
Though they come back and cannot tell the world.
My works are nearer heaven, but I sit here.
The sudden blood of these men! at a word –
Praise them, it boils, or blame them, it boils too.
I, painting from myself and to myself,
Know what I do, am unmoved by men's blame
Or their praise either. Somebody remarks
Morello's outline there is wrongly traced,
His hue mistaken; what of that? or else,
Rightly traced and well ordered; what of that?
Speak as they please, what does the mountain care?
Ah, but a man's reach should exceed his grasp,

Or what's a heaven for? All is silver-grey
Placid and perfect with my art: the worse!
I know both what I want and what might gain,
And yet how profitless to know, to sigh
'Had I been two, another and myself,
Our head would have o'erlooked the world!' No doubt.
Yonder's a work now, of that famous youth
The Urbinate who died five years ago.
('Tis copied, George Vasari sent it me.)
Well, I can fancy how he did it all,
Pouring his soul, with kings and popes to see,
Reaching, that heaven might so replenish him,
Above and through his art – for it gives way;
That arm is wrongly put – and there again –
A fault to pardon in the drawing's lines,
Its body, so to speak: its soul is right,
He means right – that, a child may understand.
Still, what an arm! and I could alter it:
But all the play, the insight and the stretch –
Out of me, out of me! And wherefore out?
Had you enjoined them on me, given me soul,
We might have risen to Rafael, I and you!
Nay, Love, you did give all I asked, I think –
More than I merit, yes, by many times.
But had you – oh, with the same perfect brow,
And perfect eyes, and more than perfect mouth,
And the low voice my soul hears, as a bird
The fowler's pipe, and follows to the snare –
Had you, with these the same, but brought a mind!
Some women do so. Had the mouth there urged
'God and the glory! never care for gain.
The present by the future, what is that?
Live for fame, side by side with Agnolo!
Rafael is waiting: up to God, all three!'
I might have done it for you. So it seems:

Perhaps not. All is as God over-rules.
Beside, incentives come from the soul's self;
The rest avail not. Why do I need you?
What wife had Rafael, or has Agnolo?
In this world, who can do a thing, will not;
And who would do it, cannot, I perceive:
Yet the will's somewhat – somewhat, too, the power –
And thus we half-men struggle. At the end,
God, I conclude, compensates, punishes.
'Tis safer for me, if the award be strict,
That I am something underrated here,
Poor this long while, despised, to speak the truth.
I dared not, do you know, leave home all day,
For fear of chancing on the Paris lords.
The best is when they pass and look aside;
But they speak sometimes; I must bear it all.
Well may they speak! That Francis, that first time,
And that long festal year at Fontainebleau!
I surely then could sometimes leave the ground,
Put on the glory, Rafael's daily wear,
In that humane great monarch's golden look, –
One finger in his beard or twisted curl
Over his mouth's good mark that made the smile,
One arm about my shoulder, round my neck,
The jingle of his gold chain in my ear,
I painting proudly with his breath on me,
All his court round him, seeing with his eyes,
Such frank French eyes, and such a fire of souls
Profuse, my hand kept plying by those hearts, –
And, best of all, this, this, this face beyond,
This in the background, waiting on my work,
To crown the issue with a last reward!
A good time, was it not, my kingly days?
And had you not grown restless . . . but I know –
'Tis done and past; 'twas right, my instinct said;

Too live the life grew, golden and not grey,
And I'm the weak-eyed bat no sun should tempt
Out of the grange whose four walls make his world.
How could it end in any other way?
You called me, and I came home to your heart.
The triumph was – to reach and stay there; since
I reached it ere the triumph, what is lost?
Let my hands frame your face in your hair's gold,
You beautiful Lucrezia that are mine!
'Rafael did this, Andrea painted that;
The Roman's is the better when you pray,
But still the other's Virgin was his wife –'
Men will excuse me. I am glad to judge
Both pictures in your presence; clearer grows
My better fortune, I resolve to think.
For, do you know, Lucrezia, as God lives,
Said one day Agnolo, his very self,
To Rafael . . . I have known it all these years . . .
(When the young man was flaming out his thoughts
Upon a palace-wall for Rome to see,
Too lifted up in heart because of it)
'Friend, there's a certain sorry little scrub
Goes up and down our Florence, none cares how,
Who, were he set to plan and execute
As you are, pricked on by your popes and kings,
Would bring the sweat into that brow of yours!'
To Rafael's! – and indeed the arm is wrong.
I hardly dare . . . yet, only you to see,
Give the chalk here – quick, thus the line should go!
Ay, but the soul! he's Rafael! rub it out!
Still, all I care for, if he spoke the truth,
(What he? why, who but Michel Agnolo?
Do you forget already words like those?)
If really there was such a chance, so lost, –
Is, whether you're – not grateful – but more pleased.

Well, let me think so. And you smile indeed!
This hour has been an hour! Another smile?
If you would sit thus by me every night
I should work better, do you comprehend?
I mean that I should earn more, give you more.
See, it is settled dusk now; there's a star;
Morello's gone, the watch-lights show the wall,
The cue-owls speak the name we call them by.
Come from the window, love, – come in, at last,
Inside the melancholy little house
We built to be so gay with. God is just.
King Francis may forgive me: oft at nights
When I look up from painting, eyes tired out,
The walls become illumined, brick from brick
Distinct, instead of mortar, fierce bright gold,
That gold of his I did cement them with!
Let us but love each other. Must you go?
That Cousin here again? he waits outside?
Must see you – you, and not with me? Those loans?
More gaming debts to pay? you smiled for that?
Well, let smiles buy me! have you more to spend?
While hand and eye and something of a heart
Are left me, work's my ware, and what's it worth?
I'll pay my fancy. Only let me sit
The grey remainder of the evening out,
Idle, you call it, and muse perfectly
How I could paint, were I but back in France,
One picture, just one more – the Virgin's face,
Not yours this time! I want you at my side
To hear them – that is, Michel Agnolo –
Judge all I do and tell you of its worth.
Will you? Tomorrow, satisfy your friend.
I take the subjects for his corridor,
Finish the portrait out of hand – there, there,
And throw him in another thing or two

If he demurs; the whole should prove enough
To pay for this same Cousin's freak. Beside,
What's better and what's all I care about,
Get you the thirteen scudi for the ruff!
Love, does that please you? Ah, but what does he,
The Cousin! what does he to please you more?

I am grown peaceful as old age tonight.
I regret little, I would change still less.
Since there my past life lies, why alter it?
The very wrong to Francis! – it is true
I took his coin, was tempted and complied,
And built this house and sinned, and all is said.
My father and my mother died of want.
Well, had I riches of my own? you see
How one gets rich! Let each one bear his lot.
They were born poor, lived poor, and poor they died:
And I have laboured somewhat in my time
And not been paid profusely. Some good son
Paint my two hundred pictures – let him try!
No doubt, there's something strikes a balance. Yes,
You loved me quite enough, it seems tonight.
This must suffice me here. What would one have?
In heaven, perhaps, new chances, one more chance –
Four great walls in the New Jerusalem,
Meted on each side by the angel's reed,
For Leonard, Rafael, Agnolo and me
To cover – the three first without a wife,
While I have mine! So – still they overcome
Because there's still Lucrezia, – as I choose.

Again the Cousin's whistle! Go, my Love.

The Lost Leader

I

Just for a handful of silver he left us,
  Just for a riband to stick in his coat –
Found the one gift of which fortune bereft us,
  Lost all the others she lets us devote;
They, with the gold to give, doled him out silver,
  So much was theirs who so little allowed:
How all our copper had gone for his service!
  Rags – were they purple, his heart had been proud!
We that had loved him so, followed him, honoured him,
  Lived in his mild and magnificent eye,
Learned his great language, caught his clear accents,
  Made him our pattern to live and to die!
Shakespeare was of us, Milton was for us,
  Burns, Shelley, were with us – they watch from their graves!
He alone breaks from the van and the freemen,
  He alone sinks to the rear and the slaves!

II

We shall march prospering, – not through his presence;
  Songs may inspirit us, – not from his lyre;
Deeds will be done, – while he boasts his quiescence,
  Still bidding crouch whom the rest bade aspire:
Blot out his name, then, record one lost soul more,
  One task more declined, one more footpath untrod,
One more devils'-triumph and sorrow for angels,
  One wrong more to man, one more insult to God!
Life's night begins: let him never come back to us!

There would be doubt, hesitation and pain,
Forced praise on our part – the glimmer of twilight,
   Never glad confident morning again!
Best fight on well, for we taught him – strike gallantly,
   Menace our heart ere we master his own;
Then let him receive the new knowledge and wait us,
   Pardoned in heaven, the first by the throne!

Memorabilia

I
Ah, did you once see Shelley plain,
   And did he stop and speak to you
And did you speak to him again?
   How strange it seems and new!

II
But you were living before that,
   And also you are living after;
And the memory I started at –
   My starting moves your laughter.

III
I crossed a moor, with a name of its own
   And a certain use in the world no doubt,
Yet a hand's-breadth of it shines alone
   'Mid the blank miles round about:

IV
For there I picked up on the heather
   And there I put inside my breast
A moulted feather, an eagle-feather!
   Well, I forget the rest.

'How They Brought the Good News from Ghent to Aix'

I

I sprang to the stirrup, and Joris, and he;
I galloped, Dirck galloped, we galloped all three;
'Good speed!' cried the watch, as the gate-bolts undrew;
'Speed!' echoed the wall to us galloping through;
Behind shut the postern, the lights sank to rest,
And into the midnight we galloped abreast.

II

Not a word to each other; we kept the great pace
Neck by neck, stride by stride, never changing our place;
I turned in my saddle and made its girths tight,
Then shortened each stirrup, and set the pique right,
Rebuckled the cheek-strap, chained slacker the bit,
Nor galloped less steadily Roland a whit.

III

'Twas moonset at starting; but while we drew near
Lokeren, the cocks crew and twilight dawned clear;
At Boom, a great yellow star came out to see;
At Düffeld, 'twas morning as plain as could be;
And from Mecheln church-steeple we heard the half-chime,
So, Joris broke silence with, 'Yet there is time!'

IV

At Aershot, up leaped of a sudden the sun,
And against him the cattle stood black every one,
To stare through the mist at us galloping past,
And I saw my stout galloper Roland at last,

With resolute shoulders, each butting away
The haze, as some bluff river headland its spray:

V

And his low head and crest, just one sharp ear bent back
For my voice, and the other pricked out on his track;
And one eye's black intelligence, – ever that glance
O'er its white edge at me, his own master, askance!
And the thick heavy spume-flakes which aye and anon
His fierce lips shook upwards in galloping on.

VI

By Hasselt, Dirck groaned; and cried Joris, 'Stay spur!
Your Roos galloped bravely, the fault's not in her,
We'll remember at Aix' – for one heard the quick wheeze
Of her chest, saw the stretched neck and staggering knees,
And sunk tail, and horrible heave of the flank,
As down on her haunches she shuddered and sank.

VII

So, we were left galloping, Joris and I,
Past Looz and past Tongres, no cloud in the sky;
The broad sun above laughed a pitiless laugh,
'Neath our feet broke the brittle bright stubble like chaff;
Till over by Dalhem a dome-spire sprang white,
And 'Gallop,' gasped Joris, 'for Aix is in sight!'

VIII

'How they'll greet us!' – and all in a moment his roan
Rolled neck and croup over, lay dead as a stone;
And there was my Roland to bear the whole weight
Of the news which alone could save Aix from her fate,
With his nostrils like pits full of blood to the brim,
And with circles of red for his eye-sockets' rim.

IX

Then I cast loose my buffcoat, each holster let fall,
Shook off both my jack-boots, let go belt and all,
Stood up in the stirrup, leaned, patted his ear,
Called my Roland his pet-name, my horse without peer;
Clapped my hands, laughed and sang, any noise, bad or good,
Till at length into Aix Roland galloped and stood.

X

And all I remember is – friends flocking round
As I sat with his head 'twixt my knees on the ground;
And no voice but was praising this Roland of mine,
As I poured down his throat our last measure of wine,
Which (the burgesses voted by common consent)
Was no more than his due who brought good news from Ghent.

The Patriot

An Old Story

I

It was roses, roses, all the way,
  With myrtle mixed in my path like mad:
The house-roofs seemed to heave and sway,
  The church-spires flamed, such flags they had,
A year ago on this very day.

II

The air broke into a mist with bells,
  The old walls rocked with the crowd and cries.
Had I said, 'Good folk, mere noise repels –
  But give me your sun from yonder skies!'
They had answered, 'And afterward, what else?'

III

Alack, it was I who leaped at the sun
  To give it my loving friends to keep!
Naught man could do, have I left undone:
  And you see my harvest, what I reap
This very day, now a year is run.

IV

There's nobody on the house-tops now –
  Just a palsied few at the windows set;
For the best of the sight is, all allow,
  At the Shambles' Gate – or, better yet,
By the very scaffold's foot, I trow.

V

I go in the rain, and, more than needs,
　　A rope cuts both my wrists behind;
And I think, by the feel, my forehead bleeds,
　　For they fling, whoever has a mind,
Stones at me for my year's misdeeds.

VI

Thus I entered, and thus I go!
　　In triumphs, people have dropped down dead.
'Paid by the world, what dost thou owe
　　Me?' – God might question; now instead,
'Tis God shall repay: I am safer so.

Prospice

Fear death? – to feel the fog in my throat,
    The mist in my face,
When the snows begin, and the blasts denote
    I am nearing the place,
The power of the night, the press of the storm,
    The post of the foe;
Where he stands, the Arch Fear in a visible form,
    Yet the strong man must go:
For the journey is done and the summit attained.
    And the barriers fall,
Though a battle's to fight ere the guerdon be gained,
    The reward of it all.
I was ever a fighter, so – one fight more,
    The best and the last!
I would hate that death bandaged my eyes, and forebore,
    And bade me creep past.
No! let me taste the whole of it, fare like my peers
    The heroes of old,
Bear the brunt, in a minute pay glad life's arrears
    Of pain, darkness and cold.
For sudden the worst turns the best to the brave,
    The black minute's at end,
And the elements' rage, the fiend-voices that rave,
    Shall dwindle, shall blend,
Shall change, shall become first a peace out of pain,
    Then a light, then thy breast,
O thou soul of my soul! I shall clasp thee again,
    And with God be the rest!

LORD BYRON

George Gordon Byron, Lord Byron (he inherited the title at the age of ten) was born in London in 1788. A poet, playwright, essayist and campaigner for Liberal causes, he exerted a profound influence on Romanticism. His collection *Childe Harold's Pilgrimage*, the first cantos of which were published in 1812, brought him worldwide fame. His satirical and controversial masterpiece *Don Juan* was published in 1819. He died of fever at Missolonghi in 1824 during his campaign for Greek independence.

LORD BYRON

Not Laughing But Weeping

'I will cut a swathe through the world or perish in the attempt': Byron, aged sixteen. Well, he cut a swathe through the world and perished in the attempt. He died, one of the most celebrated poets in Europe and the most infamous in England, aged thirty-six, a hero and a soldier fighting for Greek independence. It was an act of remarkable courage and self-sacrifice. The historian Macaulay coupled Byron's name with the hero of his youth, Napoleon: 'Two men have died within our recollection, who had raised themselves, each in his own department, to the height of glory. One of them died at Longwood, the other at Missolonghi.' Carlyle considerd Byron 'the noblest spirit in Europe' and also linked him with Napoleon. In Bertrand Russell's *History of Western Philosophy* Byron has a chapter all to himself. The Byronic myth, in which, as John Updike says, 'the poetry projected a Personality – a personality Napoleonic in its insatiability and capacity for ruinous defeat', was to inspire painters – Delacroix, musicians – Berlioz, writers – Pushkin, Nietzsche, Goethe (who, according to the American critic Harold Bloom, developed a kind of infatuation for Byron) and the Brontës, most particularly Emily. His arrival in the world, on the twenty-second of January 1788, was as dramatic as his departure. He was born with a caul over his head and talipes (a form of club foot) to The Laird of Gight, Scots heiress Catherine Gordon, and her husband Mad Jack Byron. Jack Byron, father of Byron's half-sister Augusta from his previous marriage, squandered two matrimonial fortunes and died three years after his marriage to

Catherine, leaving her a financially embarrassed widow. Mother and child moved to Scotland and then back to England when Byron, at the age of ten, inherited the Gothic masterpiece Newstead Abbey. But north or south they were not a happy pair. There were rumours of neglect and of possible abuse by his sinister nanny May Gray. Byron was an almost pathologically shy child and became a seriously overweight adolescent. At Harrow he was cruelly mocked for his limp due to the heavy iron brace he was forced to wear under his trousers. He fought back hard, according to school friend Robert Peel, eventual creator of the Metropolitan Police. Keats, Shelley and Lowell were also playground fighters. Poetry is not for sissies. There were homosexual affairs at school, though in the holidays chaste obsessions with Mary Chaworth and Margaret Parker disturbed his family with their intensity. Dante's belief that such emotional ardour in youth often indicates exceptional artistic gifts would seem to have been true in Byron's case. The lover and fighter were fore-shadowed early.

So how did the shy, unhappy boy, the awkward, overweight ado-lescent, become the legendary Lord Byron? The world, it is said, bends to a committed will. Byron starved himself into physical beauty and became one of the great seducers of his time, of both men and women. Harold Nicolson said of him: 'he was a catalogue of false positions. His brain was male, his character was feminine'. The boy in the iron brace became a legendary swimmer, swimming the Hellespont in under two hours. The boy who cultivated the image of the dilettante and said later, 'I hate a fellow who's all author', in fact read voraciously. Before he went to Trinity, Cambridge, he boasted that he'd read more than 4000 books, including the Old Testament, the classics (particu-larly Greek tragedy), biography, history and novels and poetry, most particularly Pope, whom he idolised. Then, aged nineteen, catching life and art by the throat, he took his natural narrative gift and his astonishing fluency and dashed into poetry. 'I can never recast any-thing . . . I am like the Tiger, if I miss at first spring / I go back growling to my Jungle again – But if I *do* hit – it is crushing!'

In fact *he* was hit. His first collection, *Hours of Idleness* (1807), was cruelly savaged by the critics. Byron, badly wounded by the reviews, went back to his jungle and then pounced. With his clever satire 'English Bards and Scots Reviewers' in 1809 he mocked his enemies. In the same year he took his seat in the House of Lords, where he spoke with eloquence for Liberal causes. In 1812, after two years of extensive and sometimes dangerous travel through Spain, Malta, Armenia and Greece, Byron published the first two cantos of *Childe Harold's Pilgrimage*, and, aged only twenty-four, woke up and found himself famous. He'd invented himself, magnificently. 'It is only the self that he invented that he understood perfectly', according to Eliot. 'Lord Byron,' wrote Stendhal, 'was the unique object of his own attention.' Not quite. Critics and society now showered him with praise. He had no objection. He assiduously polished his image and acquired legions of adoring fans. Amongst them, infamously, was Lady Caroline Lamb, who, when she first saw him, turned and walked away. Alas not for long – though she wrote in her journal that evening that Lord Byron was 'mad – bad – and dangerous to know'. According to Ruskin, Byron was without mercy, perhaps because he believed that 'the great object in life is Sensation', to fill the 'craving void'. Other than his half-sister Augusta, whom he certainly loved deeply and with whom he probably had a child, and Countess Teresa Guiccioli, whom Iris Origo called 'The Last Attachment', few were left unwounded by an encounter with Byron. His wife, the cool, brilliant mathematician Annabelle Milbanke, left him within a year of marriage, taking their child (who as Ada Lovelace would, with Charles Babbage, collaborate on the early computer) amid rumours of sexual abuse within a marriage that was on occasion a bizarre *ménage à trois* with Augusta. Caroline Lamb added to the scandal when in a fit of jealous rage she implied homosexuality. The charge was serious – in 1806 there'd been six hangings; in Byron's time imprison-ment was common. He was now hounded out of England. Like Shelley, he was bitter. Like Shelley, he wrote on. His output was prodigious: plays, among them *Manfred*, *The Two Foscari*, *Werner* (translated by Goethe), an Armenian dictionary – a notoriously difficult language to master – and of course the poetry. Of Byron's final masterpiece, *Don Juan*,

Eliot said it contained a satire on English society for which he could find no parallel in English literature. 'Society,' Byron wrote, 'is now one polished horde, / Formed of two mighty tribes, the Bores and the Bored.' Though it is the most savagely witty poem in this or any language, it also warns us that 'If I laugh at any mortal thing / 'Tis that I may not weep'.

Byron's death plunged all of Greece and much of Europe into mourning. However, because of his scandalous past, he was refused burial at both Westminster Abbey and St Paul's, and was finally interred in the family vaults near Newstead Abbey. The cortège slowly made its way through towns and villages thronged with those who wished to pay tribute. As he was a peer many aristocrats sent their carriages. He was buried as a nobleman and not as a poet. He knew his country well.

The Poems

'Mr Dallas has placed in your hands a manuscript poem which he tells me you do not object to publishing.' Oh the insouciance, the sheer thrilling confidence of it! The hands were those of Mr John Murray, who with the astonishingly successful publication of *Childe Harold's Pilgrimage* embarked on one of the most turbulent literary and personal relationships between publisher and published. It would not end well. Few relationships with Byron did, and the tears were rarely his. Canto III however opens with a heartbroken lament for his daughter Ada, from whom he was parted for ever when he left England in disgrace in April 1816, 'the wandering outlaw of his own dark mind', and continues into a lament for Napoleon, 'Conqueror and captive of the earth', defeated at Waterloo on 18 June 1815. Verses thirty-six to forty-five present an unforgettable portrait of the ambition which spurs on 'the madmen who have made men mad'.

'The Destruction of Sennacherib' has a ferocious energy, the opening verse irresistible in its rhythmic power. 'Darkness', written earlier, is a surprise to those who like Byron-lite, of whom we shall drink deeply in *Don Juan*. 'Darkness' paints an almost Dantesque nightmare vision of the future. Night of course can sparkle, as did the mourning dress, decorated with spangles, of Lady Anne Wilmot. The dress and its wearer dazzled Byron when he saw her at a party. 'She walks in beauty' is a morning-after poem with a difference – it's chaste. It's also a lyrical masterpiece. 'When we two parted' is one of the great songs of lost love. It makes one weep. Alas, it's too cruel to speak the last verse, long suppressed to protect the reputation of Lady Frances (Fanny) Webster. Here it is *sotto voce*. 'Then fare thee well, Fanny / Now doubly undone / To prove false unto many / As faithless to one / Thou art past all re-calling / Even would I recall / For the woman once falling / Forever must fall.' Byron, a feminist – in his fashion! He believed, and was loathed for it, that women were as sexually voracious as men. 'I'd like to know who's been ravished,' he once cried when accused again of promiscuity. 'I've been more ravished myself than anybody since the Trojan War.' Eliot noted a certain passivity in Byron, whose letters imply that, in sexual matters, he often considered himself under obligation! He was aware however that the price for women was higher – as his lines in Julia's letter make clear: 'Man's love is of his life a thing apart, / 'Tis woman's whole existence'. *Don Juan*, his masterpiece, is full of emotion; 'The emotion is hatred. Hatred of hypocrisy', wrote Eliot. Since, however, Byron had discovered that in the *ottava rima* he could 'without straining hard to versify rattle on exactly as I talk / With anybody in a ride or walk', the delight we feel in listening to or reading *Don Juan* momentarily numbs us to its stinging truthfulness. In Canto I, a deliciously vicious marriage from hell – that of Don Juan's parents Don Jóse and Donna Inez, who wished 'each other, not divorced, but dead' – is followed later, much later, by the initially slow efforts at seduction by the adolescent Don Juan of the very pretty Julia, twenty-three and married to Don Jóse, fifty. It's so unfair that, as Byron notes, 'At *fifty* love for love is rare'. Of the poem, translated by Goethe (a fact which gave Byron considerable satisfaction), the poet declared, 'It may be profligate . . . but is it not life? Is it not the thing?' It is indeed. 'Sorrow is knowledge' he wrote in *Manfred,* and few have written a gentler, sweeter poem about the inevitable than Byron's 'So, we'll go no more a roving'.

Childe Harold's Pilgrimage

Canto the Third
[excerpt]

XXXVI

    There sunk the greatest, nor the worst of men,
    Whose spirit antithetically mixt
    One moment of the mightiest, and again
    On little objects with like firmness fixt,
    Extreme in all things! hadst thou been betwixt,
    Thy throne had still been thine, or never been;
    For daring made thy rise as fall: thou seek'st
    Even now to re-assume the imperial mien,
And shake again the world, the Thunderer of the scene!

XXXVII

    Conqueror and captive of the earth art thou!
    She trembles at thee still, and thy wild name
    Was ne'er more bruited in men's minds than now
    That thou art nothing, save the jest of Fame,
    Who woo'd thee once, thy vassal, and became
    The flatterer of thy fierceness, till thou wert
    A god unto thyself; nor less the same
    To the astounded kingdoms all inert,
Who deem'd thee for a time whate'er thou didst assert.

XXXVIII

    Oh, more or less than man – in high or low,
    Battling with nations, flying from the field;
    Now making monarchs' necks thy footstool, now
    More than thy meanest soldier taught to yield;

An empire thou couldst crush, command, rebuild,
But govern not thy pettiest passion, nor,
However deeply in men's spirits skill'd,
Look through thine own, nor curb the lust of war,
Nor learn that tempted Fate will leave the loftiest star.

XXXIX

Yet well thy soul hath brook'd the turning tide
With that untaught innate philosophy,
Which, be it wisdom, coldness, or deep pride,
Is gall and wormwood to an enemy.
When the whole host of hatred stood hard by,
To watch and mock thee shrinking, thou hast smiled
With a sedate and all-enduring eye; –
When Fortune fled her spoil'd and favourite child,
He stood unbow'd beneath the ills upon him piled.

XL

Sager than in thy fortunes; for in them
Ambition steel'd thee on too far to show
That just habitual scorn, which could contemn
Men and their thoughts; 'twas wise to feel, not so
To wear it ever on thy lip and brow,
And spurn the instruments thou wert to use
Till they were turn'd unto thine overthrow;
'Tis but a worthless world to win or lose;
So hath it proved to thee, and all such lot who choose.

XLI

If, like a tower upon a headlong rock,
Thou hadst been made to stand or fall alone,
Such scorn of man had help'd to brave the shock;
But men's thoughts were the steps which paved thy throne,
Their admiration thy best weapon shone;

The part of Philip's son was thine, not then
  (Unless aside thy purple had been thrown)
  Like stern Diogenes to mock at men;
For sceptred cynics earth were far too wide a den.

XLII

But quiet to quick bosoms is a hell,
  And *there* hath been thy bane; there is a fire
  And motion of the soul which will not dwell
In its own narrow being, but aspire
Beyond the fitting medium of desire;
  And, but once kindled, quenchless evermore,
  Preys upon high adventure, nor can tire
Of aught but rest; a fever at the core,
Fatal to him who bears, to all who ever bore.

XLIII

This makes the madmen who have made men mad
  By their contagion; Conquerors and Kings,
  Founders of sects and systems, to whom add
Sophists, Bards, Statesmen, all unquiet things
Which stir too strongly the soul's secret springs,
  And are themselves the fools to those they fool;
  Envied, yet how unenviable! what stings
Are theirs! One breast laid open were a school
Which would unteach mankind the lust to shine or rule:

XLIV

Their breath is agitation, and their life
  A storm whereon they ride, to sink at last,
  And yet so nursed and bigoted to strife,
That should their days, surviving perils past,
Melt to calm twilight, they feel overcast
  With sorrow and supineness, and so die;

Even as a flame unfed, which runs to waste
With its own flickering, or a sword laid by,
Which eats into itself, and rusts ingloriously.

XLV

He who ascends to mountain-tops, shall find
The loftiest peaks most wrapt in clouds and snow;
He who surpasses or subdues mankind,
Must look down on the hate of those below.
Though high *above* the sun of glory glow,
And far *beneath* the earth and ocean spread,
Round him are icy rocks, and loudly blow
Contending tempests on his naked head,
And thus reward the toils which to those summits led.

The Destruction of Sennacherib

I
The Assyrian came down like the wolf on the fold,
And his cohorts were gleaming in purple and gold;
And the sheen of their spears was like stars on the sea,
When the blue wave rolls nightly on deep Galilee.

II
Like the leaves of the forest when Summer is green,
That host with their banners at sunset were seen:
Like the leaves of the forest when Autumn hath blown,
That host on the morrow lay wither'd and strown.

III
For the Angel of Death spread his wings on the blast,
And breathed in the face of the foe as he pass'd;
And the eyes of the sleepers wax'd deadly and chill,
And their hearts but once heaved, and for ever grew still!

IV
And there lay the steed with his nostril all wide,
But through it there roll'd not the breath of his pride:
And the foam of his gasping lay white on the turf,
And cold as the spray of the rock-beating surf.

V
And there lay the rider distorted and pale,
With the dew on his brow, and the rust on his mail;
And the tents were all silent, the banners alone,
The lances unlifted, the trumpet unblown.

VI

And the widows of Ashur are loud in their wail,
And the idols are broke in the temple of Baal;
And the might of the Gentile, unsmote by the sword,
Hath melted like snow in the glance of the Lord!

Darkness

I had a dream, which was not all a dream.
The bright sun was extinguish'd, and the stars
Did wander darkling in the eternal space,
Rayless, and pathless, and the icy earth
Swung blind and blackening in the moonless air;
Morn came and went – and came, and brought no day,
And men forgot their passions in the dread
Of this their desolation; and all hearts
Were chill'd into a selfish prayer for light:
And they did live by watchfires – and the thrones,
The palaces of crowned kings – the huts,
The habitations of all things which dwell,
Were burnt for beacons; cities were consumed,
And men were gather'd round their blazing homes
To look once more into each other's face;
Happy were those who dwelt within the eye
Of the volcanos, and their mountain-torch:
A fearful hope was all the world contain'd;
Forests were set on fire – but hour by hour
They fell and faded – and the crackling trunks
Extinguish'd with a crash – and all was black.
The brows of men by the despairing light
Wore an unearthly aspect, as by fits
The flashes fell upon them; some lay down
And hid their eyes and wept; and some did rest
Their chins upon their clenched hands, and smiled;
And others hurried to and fro, and fed
Their funeral piles with fuel, and look'd up

With mad disquietude on the dull sky,
The pall of a past world; and then again
With curses cast them down upon the dust,
And gnash'd their teeth and howl'd: the wild birds shriek'd,
And, terrified, did flutter on the ground,
And flap their useless wings; the wildest brutes
Came tame and tremulous; and vipers crawl'd
And twined themselves among the multitude,
Hissing, but stingless – they were slain for food:
And War, which for a moment was no more,
Did glut himself again; – a meal was bought
With blood, and each sate sullenly apart
Gorging himself in gloom: no love was left;
All earth was but one thought – and that was death,
Immediate and inglorious; and the pang
Of famine fed upon all entrails – men
Died, and their bones were tombless as their flesh;
The meagre by the meagre were devour'd,
Even dogs assail'd their masters, all save one,
And he was faithful to a corse, and kept
The birds and beasts and famish'd men at bay,
Till hunger clung them, or the dropping dead
Lured their lank jaws; himself sought out no food,
But with a piteous and perpetual moan,
And a quick desolate cry, licking the hand
Which answer'd not with a caress – he died.
The crowd was famish'd by degrees; but two
Of an enormous city did survive,
And they were enemies: they met beside
The dying embers of an altar-place
Where had been heap'd a mass of holy things
For an unholy usage; they raked up,
And shivering scraped with their cold skeleton hands
The feeble ashes, and their feeble breath
Blew for a little life, and made a flame

Which was a mockery; then they lifted up
Their eyes as it grew lighter, and beheld
Each other's aspects – saw, and shriek'd, and died –
Even of their mutual hideousness they died,
Unknowing who he was upon whose brow
Famine had written Fiend. The world was void,
The populous and the powerful was a lump,
Seasonless, herbless, treeless, manless, lifeless –
A lump of death – a chaos of hard clay.
The rivers, lakes, and ocean all stood still,
And nothing stirr'd within their silent depths;
Ships sailorless lay rotting on the sea,
And their masts fell down piecemeal; as they dropp'd
They slept on the abyss without a surge –
The waves were dead; the tides were in their grave,
The Moon, their mistress, had expired before;
The winds were wither'd in the stagnant air,
And the clouds perish'd; Darkness had no need
Of aid from them – She was the Universe.

Diodati, July, 1816

She walks in beauty

I

She walks in beauty, like the night
   Of cloudless climes and starry skies;
And all that's best of dark and bright
   Meet in her aspect and her eyes:
Thus mellow'd to that tender light
   Which heaven to gaudy day denies.

II

One shade the more, one ray the less,
   Had half impair'd the nameless grace
Which waves in every raven tress,
   Or softly lightens o'er her face;
Where thoughts serenely sweet express
   How pure, how dear their dwelling-place.

III

And on that cheek, and o'er that brow,
   So soft, so calm, yet eloquent,
The smiles that win, the tints that glow,
   But tell of days in goodness spent,
A mind at peace with all below,
   A heart whose love is innocent!

When we two parted

When we two parted
  In silence and tears,
Half broken-hearted
  To sever for years,
Pale grew thy cheek and cold,
  Colder thy kiss;
Truly that hour foretold
  Sorrow to this.

The dew of the morning
  Sunk chill on my brow –
It felt like the warning
  Of what I feel now.
Thy vows are all broken,
  And light is thy fame;
I hear thy name spoken,
  And share in its shame.

They name thee before me,
  A knell to mine ear;
A shudder comes o'er me –
  Why wert thou so dear?
They know not I knew thee,
  Who knew thee too well: –
Long, long shall I rue thee,
  Too deeply to tell.

LORD BYRON

In secret we met –
    In silence I grieve,
That thy heart could forget,
    Thy spirit deceive.
If I should meet thee
    After long years,
How should I greet thee? –
    With silence and tears.

Don Juan

Canto One
[excerpts]

9

His father's name was Jóse – *Don*, of course,
    A true Hidalgo, free from every stain
Of Moor or Hebrew blood, he traced his source
    Through the most Gothic gentlemen of Spain;
A better cavalier ne'er mounted horse,
    Or, being mounted, e'er got down again,
Than Jóse, who begot our hero, who
Begot – but that's to come – Well, to renew:

10

His mother was a learned lady, famed
    For every branch of every science known –
In every Christian language ever named,
    With virtues equall'd by her wit alone,
She made the cleverest people quite ashamed,
    And even the good with inward envy groan,
Finding themselves so very much exceeded
In their own way by all the things that she did.

15

Some women use their tongues – she look'd a lecture,
    Each eye a sermon, and her brow a homily,
An all-in-all-sufficient self-director,
    Like the lamented late Sir Samuel Romilly,
The Law's expounder, and the State's corrector
    Whose suicide was almost an anomaly –

One sad example more, that 'All is vanity', –
(The jury brought their verdict in 'Insanity').

18
Perfect she was, but as perfection is
    Insipid in this naughty world of ours,
Where our first parents never learn'd to kiss
    Till they were exiled from their earlier bowers,
Where all was peace, and innocence, and bliss,
    (I wonder how they got through the twelve hours)
Don Jóse, like a lineal son of Eve,
Went plucking various fruit without her leave.

19
He was a mortal of the careless kind,
    With no great love for learning, or the learn'd,
Who chose to go where'er he had a mind,
    And never dream'd his lady was concern'd;
The world, as usual, wickedly inclined
    To see a kingdom or a house o'erturn'd,
Whisper'd he had a mistress, some said *two*,
But for domestic quarrels *one* will do.

22
'Tis pity learned virgins ever wed
    With persons of no sort of education,
Or gentlemen, who, though well-born and -bred,
    Grow tired of scientific conversation:
I don't choose to say much upon this head,
    I'm a plain man, and in a single station,
But – Oh! ye lords of ladies intellectual,
Inform us truly, have they not hen-peck'd you all?

23

Don Jóse and his lady quarrell'd – *why*,
  Not any of the many could divine,
Though several thousand people chose to try,
  'Twas surely no concern of theirs nor mine;
I loathe that low vice curiosity,
  But if there's any thing in which I shine
'Tis in arranging all my friends' affairs
Not having, of my own, domestic cares.

26

Don Jóse and the Donna Inez led
  For some time an unhappy sort of life,
Wishing each other, not divorced, but dead;
  They lived respectably as man and wife,
Their conduct was exceedingly well-bred,
  And gave no outward signs of inward strife,
Until at length the smother'd fire broke out,
And put the business past all kind of doubt.

27

For Inez call'd some druggists and physicians,
  And tried to prove her loving lord was *mad*,
But as he had some lucid intermissions,
  She next decided he was only *bad*;
Yet when they ask'd her for her depositions,
  No sort of explanation could be had,
Save that her duty both to man and God
Required this conduct – which seem'd very odd.

28

She kept a journal, where his faults were noted,
  And open'd certain trunks of books and letters,
All which might, if occasion served, be quoted;
  And then she had all Seville for abettors,

Besides her good old grandmother (who doted);
   The hearers of her case became repeaters,
Then advocates, inquisitors, and judges,
Some for amusement, others for old grudges.

29

And then this best and meekest woman bore
   With such serenity her husband's woes,
Just as the Spartan ladies did of yore,
   Who saw their spouses kill'd, and nobly chose
Never to say a word about them more –
   Calmly she heard each calumny that rose,
And saw his agonies with such sublimity,
That all the world exclaim'd, 'What magnanimity!'

30

No doubt, this patience, when the world is damning us,
   Is philosophic in our former friends;
'Tis also pleasant to be deem'd magnanimous,
   The more so in obtaining our own ends;
And what the lawyers call a '*malus animus*',
   Conduct like this by no means comprehends:
Revenge in person's certainly no virtue,
But then 'tis not *my* fault, if *others* hurt you.

31

And if our quarrels should rip up old stories,
   And help them with a lie or two additional,
I'm not to blame, as you well know, no more is
   Any one else – they were become traditional;
Besides, their resurrection aids our glories
   By contrast, which is what we just were wishing all:
And science profits by this resurrection –
Dead scandals form good subjects for dissection.

32

Their friends had tried at reconciliation,
    Then their relations, who made matters worse;
('Twere hard to say upon a like occasion
    To whom it may be best to have recourse –
I can't say much for friend or yet relation):
    The lawyers did their utmost for divorce,
But scarce a fee was paid on either side
Before, unluckily, Don José died.

            . . .

65

Alfonso was the name of Julia's lord,
    A man well looking for his years, and who
Was neither much beloved, nor yet abhorr'd;
    They lived together as most people do,
Suffering each other's foibles by accord,
    And not exactly either *one* or *two*
Yet he was jealous, though he did not show it,
For jealousy dislikes the world to know it.

69

Juan she saw, and, as a pretty child,
    Caress'd him often, such a thing might be
Quite innocently done, and harmless styled,
    When she had twenty years, and thirteen he;
But I am not so sure I should have smiled
    When he was sixteen, Julia twenty-three,
These few short years make wondrous alterations,
Particularly amongst sun-burnt nations.

81

Love, then, but love within its proper limits,
    Was Julia's innocent determination
In young Don Juan's favour, and to him its

Exertion might be useful on occasion;
And, lighted at too pure a shrine to dim its
    Etherial lustre, with what sweet persuasion
He might be taught, by love and her together –
I really don't know what, nor Julia either.

83

Her plan she deem'd both innocent and feasible,
    And, surely, with a stripling of sixteen
Not scandal's fangs could fix on much that's seizable,
    Or if they did so, satisfied to mean
Nothing but what was good, her breast was peaceable –
    A quiet conscience makes one so serene!
Christians have burnt each other, quite persuaded
That all the Apostles would have done as they did.

84

And if in the mean time her husband died,
    But heaven forbid that such a thought should cross
Her brain, though in a dream! (and then she sigh'd)
    Never could she survive that common loss;
But just suppose that moment should betide,
    I only say suppose it – *inter nos* –
(This should be *entre nous*, for Julia thought
In French, but then the rhyme would go for nought).

99

A real husband always is suspicious,
    But still no less suspects in the wrong place,
Jealous of some one who had no such wishes,
    Or pandering blindly to his own disgrace
By harbouring some dear friend extremely vicious;
    The last indeed's infallibly the case:
And when the spouse and friend are gone off wholly,
He wonders at their vice, and not his folly.

100

Thus parents also are at times short-sighted;
    Though watchful as the lynx, they ne'er discover,
The while the wicked world beholds delighted,
    Young Hopeful's mistress, or Miss Fanny's lover,
Till some confounded escapade has blighted
    The plan of twenty years, and all is over;
And then the mother cries, the father swears,
And wonders why the devil he got heirs.

102

It was upon a day, a summer's day; –
    Summer's indeed a very dangerous season,
And so is spring about the end of May;
    The sun, no doubt, is the prevailing reason;
But whatsoe'er the cause is, one may say,
    And stand convicted of more truth than treason,
That there are months which nature grows more merry in,
March has its hares, and May must have its heroine.

105

She sate, but not alone; I know not well
    How this same interview had taken place,
And even if I knew, I should not tell –
    People should hold their tongues in any case;
No matter how or why the thing befell,
    But there were she and Juan, face to face –
When two such faces are so, 'twould be wise,
But very difficult, to shut their eyes.

106

How beautiful she look'd! her conscious heart
    Glow'd in her cheek, and yet she felt no wrong.
Oh Love! how perfect is thy mystic art,
    Strengthening the weak, and trampling on the strong,

How self-deceitful is the sagest part
 Of mortals whom thy lure hath led along –
The precipice she stood on was immense,
So was her creed in her own innocence.

107
She thought of her own strength, and Juan's youth,
 And of the folly of all prudish fears,
Victorious virtue, and domestic truth,
 And then of Don Alfonso's fifty years;
I wish these last had not occurr'd, in sooth,
 Because that number rarely much endears,
And through all climes, the snowy and the sunny,
Sounds ill in love, whate'er it may in money.

108
When people say, 'I've told you *fifty* times,'
 They mean to scold, and very often do;
When poets say, 'I've written *fifty* rhymes,'
 They make you dread that they'll recite them too;
In gangs of *fifty*, thieves commit their crimes;
 At *fifty* love for love is rare, 'tis true,
But then, no doubt, it equally as true is,
A good deal may be bought for *fifty* Louis.

109
Julia had honour, virtue, truth, and love,
 For Don Alfonso; and she inly swore,
By all the vows below to powers above,
 She never would disgrace the ring she wore,
Nor leave a wish which wisdom might reprove;
 And while she ponder'd this, besides much more,
One hand on Juan's carelessly was thrown,
Quite by mistake – she thought it was her own;

110

Unconsciously she lean'd upon the other,
    Which play'd within the tangles of her hair;
And to contend with thoughts she could not smother,
    She seem'd by the distraction of her air.
'Twas surely very wrong in Juan's mother
    To leave together this imprudent pair,
She who for many years had watch'd her son so –
I'm very certain *mine* would not have done so.

111

The hand which still held Juan's, by degrees
    Gently, but palpably confirm'd its grasp,
And if it said 'detain me, if you please';
    Yet there's no doubt she only meant to clasp
His fingers with a pure Platonic squeeze;
    She would have shrunk as from a toad, or asp,
Had she imagined such a thing could rouse
A feeling dangerous to a prudent spouse.

115

And Julia sate with Juan, half embraced
    And half retiring from the glowing arm,
Which trembled like the bosom where 'twas placed;
    Yet still she must have thought there was no harm,
Or else 'twere easy to withdraw her waist;
    But then the situation had its charm,
And then – God knows what next, – I can't go on;
I'm almost sorry that I e'er begun.

117

And Julia's voice was lost, except in sighs,
    Until too late for useful conversation;
The tears were gushing from her gentle eyes,
    I wish, indeed, they had not had occasion,

But who, alas! can love, and then be wise?
    Not that remorse did not oppose temptation,
A little still she strove, and much repented,
And whispering 'I will ne'er consent' – consented.

So, we'll go no more a roving

I
So, we'll go no more a roving
    So late into the night,
Though the heart be still as loving,
    And the moon be still as bright.

II
For the sword outwears its sheath,
    And the soul wears out the breast,
And the heart must pause to breathe,
    And love itself have rest.

III
Though the night was made for loving,
    And the day returns too soon,
Yet we'll go no more a roving
    By the light of the moon.

ROBERT FROST

Robert Lee Frost was born in San Francisco in 1874.
In 1912 he moved to England where his first volumes of
poems, *A Boy's Will* (1913) and *North of Boston* (1914),
were published to great acclaim. Over a long career
he published *Mountain Interval* (1916), *New Hampshire*
(1923), *Collected Poems* (1930), *A Witness Tree* (1942)
and *In the Clearing* (1962). He won four Pulitzer Prizes –
a record that still stands. He died in1963.

ROBERT FROST

The Poet of Terror

On 26 March 1959 a dinner was held at the Waldorf Astoria in New York to honour, on his eighty-fifth birthday, Robert Frost. This literary icon, who many believed wrote of old pieties, old virtues, was the winner of four Pulitzer Prizes – a record which still stands. Lionel Trilling the eminent critic rose to speak: 'I have to say that my Frost . . . is not the Frost I seem to perceive in the minds of so many of his admirers. He is not the Frost who reassures us by his affirmation of old virtues, old simplicities and ways of feeling; he is anything but. Frost's best poems represent the terrible actualities of life. In sum, he is a terrifying poet.' Frost was disconcerted. The audience was disconcerted. Trilling left almost immediately – but Trilling was right. For beneath the guise of the avuncular, Robert Frost was indeed the poet of terror. He was also the poet of courage; he needed it – 'I'd rather be taken for brave than anything else.' His was a life that had not only a tough beginning but one in which he later suffered a Job-like series of tragedies that would have felled all but the bravest. A poem, he wrote, 'begins in delight and ends in wisdom' and in his case the wisdom was dearly bought. He was indeed 'acquainted with the night'.

He was born in San Francisco in 1874 to William Frost, a Harvard-educated journalist and aspiring politician from the East Coast who'd gone West to pursue his ambitions. These, alas, came to nothing. He died aged thirty-four, a gambler and an alcoholic. After funeral expenses his wife, Belle, a teacher and a published poet of Scottish descent (whose family history was overshadowed by the mental ill-ness of which Frost had a deep fear) was left with only eight dollars in the bank. She had no alternative but to take her two children, Robbie and Jeanie, back to her parents-in-law in Boston, where she would resume her schoolteaching career. Frost often helped her in class and, when he could, financially, with work on farms and in factories. He wanted more: 'Inflexible ambition trains us best.' It was, in Frost's case, combined with academic brilliance and a passion for poetry inherited from his mother, as well as for the classics. According to John Updike, Frost, who won a scholarship to Dartmouth and eventually went to Harvard, knew more Greek and Latin than either Eliot or Pound. Yet Frost's poetry is almost devoid of overt classical references. However, in his monologues (and he is as great a mono-logist as Browning, with a similar genius for creating character) it is possible to trace a form of Greek tragedy in his tales of lives broken by arbitrary fate. His disturbing desire and capacity to 'trip the reader head foremost into the boundless . . . Forward, you understand, and in the dark' is clear also in the shorter poems, as in 'Bereft' and 'Fire and Ice'. Joseph Brodsky said 'Frost's is a signal from a far-distant sta-tion . . . the fuel – grief and reason.' The initial signal came in 1894 with the innocently titled 'My Butterfly', the writing of which he said was like 'cutting along a nerve'. It was his first published poem, appearing in the prestigious *Independent* newspaper. The editor noted that 'there is a secret genius between the lines'. Frost now determined on poetry for life. His previously parsimonious grandfather offered to support him for one year. No, said Frost, it will take me twenty. It did. He supported himself by farming, eventually selling his farm in Derry, New Hampshire, and, after moving to Britain, buying one in Buckinghamshire. It was in England that his first collection *A Boy's Will* was published in 1913, followed a year later by *North of Boston*, to great acclaim. Frost returned to America in his forties and from then on there was no stopping him. He would, even in late life, attract audiences numbering in their thousands. The cool Miss Marianne Moore, not given to hyperbole, said he was the best speaker she had ever heard; Alan Ginsberg said Robert Frost literally created the audience for poetry readings. 'I teach myself,' Frost said, 'my own take on the world'; and 'I sit there radiating poetry.'

It was not to be his only stage. Though he was orthodox in politics – a Liberal, he believed, was someone who wouldn't take his own side in an argument – President Kennedy invited him to read at his inauguration. Frost recited from memory a poem he had written twenty years earlier, 'The Gift Outright'. The glare of the sun had made it impossible for him to read his new poem. In 1962, Kennedy, astonishingly, asked Frost to visit Khrushchev in Moscow to plead against the construction of the Berlin Wall. It didn't work. That his intervention had been sought at all is testimony to how far he'd come.

On his deathbed Frost said, 'Love is all. Romantic love – as in stories and poems. I tremble with it.' 'The Figure a Poem Makes' is, according to his famous essay, 'the same as for love'. Love brought him Elinor White, whom he'd pursued with almost overwhelming passion, once becoming so distraught when he sensed rejection that he went missing for days in the dangerous Virginia swamps. Finally, reader, he married her. She was twenty-three and he was twenty-one. Family life brought neither of them any luck. Their son Eliott died when he was four, a daughter in infancy and another, Marjorie, having successfully fought off serious mental illness (a maternal genetic inheritance), succumbed to puerperal fever with her first child. In 1938 his beloved Elinor died. He was literally mad with grief. This is his Lear-like description: 'I can't touch my mind with a memory of any kind. I can't touch my skin.' He was consumed with guilt: 'She was too frail' for the life he'd given her due to his ruthless ambition, too many children. In a shocking line he wrote, 'God damn me when he gets around to it.' His suffering was not over, for two years later his son Carl shot himself. 'I feel,' he said, 'as though I am laid out upon a cross.' He died on 28 January 1963, aged eighty-eight: 'I would have written of me on my stone: I had a lover's quarrel with the world.' Only a man who'd carved grace out of tragedy could have written a line of such irony and sweetness.

The Poems

'If [when] you read my poem – you heard a voice, that would be to my liking . . . the gold in the ore is the sound.' Few poets believed more passionately in the sound of sense; few had a more finely attuned ear to the sense of sound. In Frost's extraordinary 'A Servant to Servants' the woman's voice is weighted, awkwardly heavy with a life of exhausted love and resignation. The line, repeated, 'I don't know' is in perfect contradictory balance with the familiar beat of her daily rhythm of duty. All is set – in an almost throwaway sequence – against the shattering perspective of family madness.

'"Out, Out—"' shocks on every level. It tells the true story of the death of a neighbour's child in a sawmill, the awful imagery of the boy's arm leaping away towards the saw, 'Neither refused the meeting'. The last line is one of literature's most savage – 'And they, since they / Were not the one dead, turned to their affairs.'

Frost wrote, 'Before I built a wall I'd ask to know / What I was walling in or walling out'. It was with considerable cunning that he recited 'Mending Wall' at an official dinner in Moscow. 'Mending Wall' is, on the surface, a poem of simple verities. However Frost, the master of metaphor, was saying something profound concerning boundaries. He had, Heaney noted, 'an appetite for independence [which] was fierce and expressed itself in a reiterated belief in his rights to limits: his defences, his fences, his freedom were all interdependent.' These limits were perhaps essential, and driven by his fear of the abyss. Poetry, Frost once wrote, is a 'momentary stay against confusion'.

Robert Frost fell in love again, after the death of his beloved Elinor, with Kay Morrison, his beautiful, cool, much admired assistant who, alas, was married. Updike notes that it was for Kay Morrison that Frost wrote and recited in public to her one of the most enchanting love lyrics in the language, 'Never Again Would Birds' Song be the Same,' with its glorious last line: 'And to do that to birds was why she came.'

'Two Look at Two' is about lovers twinned by the vision of a deer and stag, certain that the sighting authenticates their human passion. 'Acquainted With the Night' paints a haunting internal landscape. 'The Road Not Taken' was inspired by Edward Thomas's indecision during their walks in Buckinghamshire as to which path to take – a metaphor for life. We end with 'Stopping by Woods on a Snowy Evening', its iconic last lines oft quoted by Kennedy in his speeches, who had fewer 'miles to go' than anyone would have believed possible.

A Servant to Servants

I didn't make you know how glad I was
To have you come and camp here on our land.
I promised myself to get down some day
And see the way you lived, but I don't know!
With a houseful of hungry men to feed
I guess you'd find . . . It seems to me
I can't express my feelings any more
Than I can raise my voice or want to lift
My hand (oh, I can lift it when I have to).
Did ever you feel so? I hope you never.
It's got so I don't even know for sure
Whether I *am* glad, sorry, or anything.
There's nothing but a voice-like left inside
That seems to tell me how I ought to feel,
And would feel if I wasn't all gone wrong.
You take the lake. I look and look at it.
I see it's a fair, pretty sheet of water.
I stand and make myself repeat out loud
The advantages it has, so long and narrow,
Like a deep piece of some old running river
Cut short off at both ends. It lies five miles
Straight away through the mountain notch
From the sink window where I wash the plates,
And all our storms come up toward the house,
Drawing the slow waves whiter and whiter and whiter.
It took my mind off doughnuts and soda biscuit
To step outdoors and take the water dazzle
A sunny morning, or take the rising wind

About my face and body and through my wrapper,
When a storm threatened from the Dragon's Den,
And a cold chill shivered across the lake.
I see it's a fair, pretty sheet of water,
Our Willoughby! How did you hear of it?
I expect, though, everyone's heard of it.
In a book about ferns? Listen to that!
You let things more like feathers regulate
Your going and coming. And you like it here?
I can see how you might. But I don't know!
It would be different if more people came,
For then there would be business. As it is,
The cottages Len built, sometimes we rent them,
Sometimes we don't. We've a good piece of shore
That ought to be worth something, and may yet.
But I don't count on it as much as Len.
He looks on the bright side of everything,
Including me. He thinks I'll be all right
With doctoring. But it's not medicine—
Lowe is the only doctor's dared to say so—
It's rest I want—there, I have said it out—
From cooking meals for hungry hired men
And washing dishes after them—from doing
Things over and over that just won't stay done.
By good rights I ought not to have so much
Put on me, but there seems no other way.
Len says one steady pull more ought to do it.
He says the best way out is always through.
And I agree to that, or in so far
As that I can see no way out but through—
Leastways for me—but then they'll be convinced.
It's not that Len don't want the best for me.
It was his plan our moving over in
Beside the lake from where that day I showed you
We used to live—ten miles from anywhere.

We didn't change without some sacrifice,
But Len went at it to make up the loss.
His work's a man's, of course, from sun to sun,
But he works when he works as hard as I do—
Though there's small profit in comparisons.
(Women and men will make them all the same.)
But work ain't all. Len undertakes too much.
He's into everything in town. This year
It's highways, and he's got too many men
Around him to look after that make waste.
They take advantage of him shamefully,
And proud, too, of themselves for doing so.
We have four here to board, great good-for-nothings,
Sprawling about the kitchen with their talk
While I fry their bacon. Much they care!
No more put out in what they do or say
Than if I wasn't in the room at all.
Coming and going all the time, they are:
I don't learn what their names are, let alone
Their characters, or whether they are safe
To have inside the house with doors unlocked.
I'm not afraid of them, though, if they're not
Afraid of me. There's two can play at that.
I have my fancies: it runs in the family.
My father's brother wasn't right. They kept him
Locked up for years back there at the old farm.
I've been away once—yes, I've been away.
The State Asylum. I was prejudiced;
I wouldn't have sent anyone of mine there;
You know the old idea—the only asylum
Was the poorhouse, and those who could afford,
Rather than send their folks to such a place,
Kept them at home; and it does seem more human.
But it's not so: the place is the asylum.
There they have every means proper to do with,

And you aren't darkening other people's lives—
Worse than no good to them, and they no good
To you in your condition; you can't know
Affection or the want of it in that state.
I've heard too much of the old-fashioned way.
My father's brother, he went mad quite young.
Some thought he had been bitten by a dog,
Because his violence took on the form
Of carrying his pillow in his teeth;
But it's more likely he was crossed in love,
Or so the story goes. It was some girl.
Anyway all he talked about was love.
They soon saw he would do someone a mischief
If he wa'n't kept strict watch of, and it ended
In father's building him a sort of cage,
Or room within a room, of hickory poles,
Like stanchions in the barn, from floor to ceiling,—
A narrow passage all the way around.
Anything they put in for furniture
He'd tear to pieces, even a bed to lie on.
So they made the place comfortable with straw,
Like a beast's stall, to ease their consciences.
Of course they had to feed him without dishes.
They tried to keep him clothed, but he paraded
With his clothes on his arm—all of his clothes.
Cruel—it sounds. I 'spose they did the best
They knew. And just when he was at the height,
Father and mother married, and mother came,
A bride, to help take care of such a creature,
And accommodate her young life to his.
That was what marrying father meant to her.
She had to lie and hear love things made dreadful
By his shouts in the night. He'd shout and shout
Until the strength was shouted out of him,
And his voice died down slowly from exhaustion.

He'd pull his bars apart like bow and bowstring,
And let them go and make them twang until
His hands had worn them smooth as any oxbow.
And then he'd crow as if he thought that child's play
The only fun he had. I've heard them say, though,
They found a way to put a stop to it.
He was before my time—I never saw him;
But the pen stayed exactly as it was
There in the upper chamber in the ell,
A sort of catch-all full of attic clutter.
I often think of the smooth hickory bars.
It got so I would say—you know, half fooling—
'It's time I took my turn upstairs in jail'—
Just as you will till it becomes a habit.
No wonder I was glad to get away.
Mind you, I waited till Len said the word.
I didn't want the blame if things went wrong.
I was glad though, no end, when we moved out,
And I looked to be happy, and I was,
As I said, for a while—but I don't know!
Somehow the change wore out like a prescription.
And there's more to it than just window-views
And living by a lake. I'm past such help—
Unless Len took the notion, which he won't,
And I won't ask him—it's not sure enough.
I 'spose I've got to go the road I'm going:
Other folks have to, and why shouldn't I?
I almost think if I could do like you,
Drop everything and live out on the ground—
But it might be, come night, I shouldn't like it,
Or a long rain. I should soon get enough,
And be glad of a good roof overhead.
I've lain awake thinking of you, I'll warrant,
More than you have yourself, some of these nights.
The wonder was the tents weren't snatched away

From over you as you lay in your beds.
I haven't courage for a risk like that.
Bless you, of course, you're keeping me from work,
But the thing of it is, I need to *be* kept.
There's work enough to do—there's always that;
But behind's behind. The worst that you can do
Is set me back a little more behind.
I sha'n't catch up in this world, anyway.
I'd *rather* you'd not go unless you must.

'Out, Out—'

The buzz-saw snarled and rattled in the yard
And made dust and dropped stove-length sticks of wood,
Sweet-scented stuff when the breeze drew across it.
And from there those that lifted eyes could count
Five mountain ranges one behind the other
Under the sunset far into Vermont.
And the saw snarled and rattled, snarled and rattled,
As it ran light, or had to bear a load.
And nothing happened: day was all but done.
Call it a day, I wish they might have said
To please the boy by giving him the half hour
That a boy counts so much when saved from work.
His sister stood beside them in her apron
To tell them 'Supper.' At the word, the saw,
As if to prove saws knew what supper meant,
Leaped out at the boy's hand, or seemed to leap—
He must have given the hand. However it was,
Neither refused the meeting. But the hand!
The boy's first outcry was a rueful laugh,
As he swung toward them holding up the hand
Half in appeal, but half as if to keep
The life from spilling. Then the boy saw all—
Since he was old enough to know, big boy
Doing a man's work, though a child at heart—
He saw all spoiled. 'Don't let him cut my hand off—
The doctor, when he comes. Don't let him, sister!'
So. But the hand was gone already.
The doctor put him in the dark of ether.

He lay and puffed his lips out with his breath.
And then—the watcher at his pulse took fright.
No one believed. They listened at his heart.
Little—less—nothing!—and that ended it.
No more to build on there. And they, since they
Were not the one dead, turned to their affairs.

Mending Wall

Something there is that doesn't love a wall,
That sends the frozen-ground-swell under it,
And spills the upper boulders in the sun;
And makes gaps even two can pass abreast.
The work of hunters is another thing:
I have come after them and made repair
Where they have left not one stone on a stone,
But they would have the rabbit out of hiding,
To please the yelping dogs. The gaps I mean,
No one has seen them made or heard them made,
But at spring mending-time we find them there.
I let my neighbour know beyond the hill;
And on a day we meet to walk the line
And set the wall between us once again.
We keep the wall between us as we go.
To each the boulders that have fallen to each.
And some are loaves and some so nearly balls
We have to use a spell to make them balance:
'Stay where you are until our backs are turned!'
We wear our fingers rough with handling them.
Oh, just another kind of out-door game,
One on a side. It comes to little more:
There where it is we do not need the wall:
He is all pine and I am apple orchard.
My apple trees will never get across
And eat the cones under his pines, I tell him.
He only says, 'Good fences make good neighbours.'
Spring is the mischief in me, and I wonder

If I could put a notion in his head:
'*Why* do they make good neighbours? Isn't it
Where there are cows? But here there are no cows.
Before I built a wall I'd ask to know
What I was walling in or walling out,
And to whom I was like to give offence.
Something there is that doesn't love a wall,
That wants it down.' I could say 'Elves' to him,
But it's not elves exactly, and I'd rather
He said it for himself. I see him there
Bringing a stone grasped firmly by the top
In each hand, like an old-stone savage armed.
He moves in darkness as it seems to me,
Not of woods only and the shade of trees.
He will not go behind his father's saying,
And he likes having thought of it so well
He says again, 'Good fences make good neighbours.'

Acquainted With the Night

I have been one acquainted with the night.
I have walked out in rain—and back in rain.
I have outwalked the furthest city light.

I have looked down the saddest city lane.
I have passed by the watchman on his beat
And dropped my eyes, unwilling to explain.

I have stood still and stopped the sound of feet
When far away an interrupted cry
Came over houses from another street,

But not to call me back or say good-bye;
And further still at an unearthly height,
One luminary clock against the sky

Proclaimed the time was neither wrong nor right
I have been one acquainted with the night.

Two Look at Two

Love and forgetting might have carried them
A little further up the mountain side
With night so near, but not much further up.
They must have halted soon in any case
With thoughts of the path back, how rough it was
With rock and washout, and unsafe in darkness;
When they were halted by a tumbled wall
With barbed-wire binding. They stood facing this,
Spending what onward impulse they still had
In one last look the way they must not go,
On up the failing path, where, if a stone
Or earthslide moved at night, it moved itself;
No footstep moved it. 'This is all,' they sighed,
'Good-night to woods.' But not so; there was more.
A doe from round a spruce stood looking at them
Across the wall, as near the wall as they.
She saw them in their field, they her in hers.
The difficulty of seeing what stood still,
Like some up-ended boulder split in two,
Was in her clouded eyes: they saw no fear there.
She seemed to think that two thus they were safe.
Then, as if they were something that, though strange,
She could not trouble her mind with too long,
She sighed and passed unscared along the wall.
'*This*, then, is all. What more is there to ask?'
But no, not yet. A snort to bid them wait.
A buck from round the spruce stood looking at them
Across the wall as near the wall as they.

This was an antlered buck of lusty nostril,
Not the same doe come back into her place.
He viewed them quizzically with jerks of head,
As if to ask, 'Why don't you make some motion?
Or give some sign of life? Because you can't.
I doubt if you're as living as you look.'
Thus till he had them almost feeling dared
To stretch a proffering hand—and a spell-breaking.
Then he too passed unscared along the wall.
Two had seen two, whichever side you spoke from.
'This *must* be all.' It was all. Still they stood,
A great wave from it going over them,
As if the earth in one unlooked-for favor
Had made them certain earth returned their love.

Never Again Would Birds' Song be the Same

He would declare and could himself believe
That the birds there in all the garden round
From having heard the daylong voice of Eve
Had added to their own an oversound,
Her tone of meaning but without the words.
Admittedly an eloquence so soft
Could only have had an influence on birds

When call or laughter carried it aloft.
Be that as may be, she was in their song.
Moreover her voice upon their voices crossed
Had now persisted in the woods so long
That probably it never would be lost.
Never again would birds' song be the same.
And to do that to birds was why she came.

The Road Not Taken

Two roads diverged in a yellow wood,
And sorry I could not travel both
And be one traveler, long I stood
And looked down one as far as I could
To where it bent in the undergrowth;

Then took the other, as just as fair,
And having perhaps the better claim,
Because it was grassy and wanted wear;
Though as for that the passing there
Had worn them really about the same,

And both that morning equally lay
In leaves no step had trodden black.
Oh, I kept the first for another day!
Yet knowing how way leads on to way,
I doubted if I should ever come back.

I shall be telling this with a sigh
Somewhere ages and ages hence:
Two roads diverged in a wood, and I –
I took the one less traveled by,
And that has made all the difference.

Stopping by Woods on a Snowy Evening

Whose woods these are I think I know
His house is in the village though;
He will not see me stopping here
To watch his woods fill up with snow.

My little horse must think it queer
To stop without a farmhouse near
Between the woods and frozen lake
The darkest evening of the year.

He gives his harness bells a shake
To ask if there is some mistake.
The only other sound's the sweep
Of easy wind and downy flake.

The woods are lovely, dark and deep.
But I have promises to keep,
And miles to go before I sleep,
And miles to go before I sleep.

ROBERT LOWELL

Robert Traill Spence Lowell was born into American aristocracy in Boston in 1917. His first collection, *Lord Weary's Castle*, published in 1946, brought him iconic status and won the Pulitzer Prize. His seminal work *Life Studies* was hugely influential and was followed in 1973 by *The Dolphin*, for which he was awarded his second Pulitzer Prize. He died in 1977.

ROBERT LOWELL

'My mind's not right...'

True. It was however right enough to make Robert Lowell one of America's greatest poets. 'Seeing less than others can be a great strain,' he once wrote, hinting at something deeper than myopia. 'Looking back over thirty years of published work my impression is that the thread that strings the work together is autobiography.' He could have added history, that of his family and his country – the one a shadow outline of the other. According to the critic John Bayley, 'The Lowell family itself was a more potent inspiration than any literature.' His masterpiece is *Life Studies* – they are close to home. Few parents or indeed grandparents have been more assiduously studied than those of Robert Lowell and, as in 'Dolphin' and 'Day By Day', few wives have been portrayed with quite such forensic love as those of Robert Lowell. He poses, in poetry, Cocteau's challenge: 'how far one can go too far'. And answers it thus: 'you want the reader to say, this is true' and 'to believe he was getting the *real* Robert Lowell'. It's a line in which self-granted absolution mingles with strange Pirandello-like reverberations concerning self and persona.

Who was the *real* Robert Lowell? In Lowell's case, since he was often mentally ill, the question has a tragic dimension. He was born on 1 March 1917, into American aristocracy. His family included the Cabots, who talked only to the Lowells, and the Lowells, who talked only to God. His father was Robert Traill Spence Lowell Snr, 'who hadn't a mean bone, an original bone or a funny bone in his body' –

a relative's cruel, though it would seem accurate description. His mother, whose family came over on the *Mayflower*, was the formidable Charlotte Winslow, about whom her son would write two fierce poems of love and frustration: 'To Mother' ('Becoming ourselves, / we lose our nerve for children') and the brutally titled 'Unwanted'. Charlotte was a marital manipulator par excellence: 'she saw her husband as a valet sees through a master.' She dominated him and she effectively thwarted his naval career. His father declined smiling from job to job 'until in his forties his soul went underground': Lowell's haunting description in his prose poem '91 Revere Street'. Even as a child – 'always inside me is the child who died' – he wondered, why doesn't father fight back?

Nothing was going to thwart Robert Lowell Jnr. At school he was physically powerful and psychologically manipulative. He was nicknamed Caligula, mercifully shortened to Cal. In adolescence and young manhood his rages and his recklessness were such that help was sought from Dr Merrill Moore, a poet-psychiatrist, and eventually, later, from Carl Jung: 'If your son is as you have described him, / he is an incurable schizophrenic.' Sadly, nothing could save Lowell from severe mental illness and in his thirties he would tumble into the abyss of psychosis, often hospitalised for his own protection. 'I believed I could stop cars and paralyze their forces by merely standing in the middle of the highway; that I was the reincarnation of The Holy Ghost – To have known the glory, violence and banality of such an experience is corrupting.' However, within the kingdom of poetry, perhaps Lowell sensed he would work miracles or perhaps he sensed salvation. Certainly from the moment he started writing poetry aged seventeen, encouraged by the poet-teacher Richard Eberhart, he demonstrated startling intensity and utterly determined will. When told by the initially bewildered poet Allen Tate of New Criticism fame, whom he'd followed from Harvard to Tennessee, 'we really haven't any room – you'd have to pitch a tent on the lawn', Lowell did precisely that. At Kenyon College they would analyse poetry down to its last Empsonian ambiguity. 'It's such a miracle if you get lines that are halfway right' – though miracles are often troubling and they troubled him. His poems were worked and re-worked. 'You didn't write, you *re*-wrote,' his friend Randall Jarrell commented.

In 1946 his collection *Lord Weary's Castle* was published. It was in style and content American heroic, brilliant, allusive, technically dazzling, spiritual (he'd converted to Catholicism with typical intensity) and difficult. 'The Lord survives the rainbow of His will', the famous last line of 'The Quaker Graveyard in Nantucket', challenges the reader, who is best advised to resist and simply surrender to its beauty. The collection won ecstatic reviews and the Pulitzer Prize. He was barely thirty and he'd arrived – a literary star. In fact he'd achieved notoriety some time earlier with a letter to a president. Lowell, who'd volunteered in 1941 and had been turned down due to his eyesight, was drafted in 1943. 'Dear Mr President, I very much regret that I must refuse the opportunity you have afforded me in your communication of August the 6th 1943 for service in the armed forces.' Lowell attached his Declaration of Personal Responsibility. 'We are prepared to wage war without quarter or principles to the permanent destruction of Germany and Japan. I cannot honourably participate in a war whose persecution constitutes the betrayal of my country.' It was headline news. LOWELL SCION REFUSES TO FIGHT! He was sentenced to a year and a day in the Federal Correction Centre in Danbury, prior to which he spent a few days in West Street in the cell next to Lepke of Murder, Inc. – who was eventually executed. Lepke to Lowell: 'I'm in for killing. What are you in for?' 'I'm in for refusing to kill.'

Twenty-two years later, in the sixties, Lowell's involvement in anti-Vietnam demonstrations led to another, though calmer letter to a president, Johnson this time, turning down an invitation to the White House Festival of the Arts. It was again front-page news. By then of course he was America's most celebrated and most controversial poet. The publication in 1959 of *Life Studies* was a seminal moment for Lowell and for American literature. Anna Swir, the eminent critic, has written that the first duty of the writer is to create an individual style and the second – more difficult – to destroy it. Lowell did just that. 'I'd been on tour and reading aloud and more and more

I was simplifying my poems.' They were indeed simpler, less allusive; they were also infinitely more disturbing. They inspired, among others, Sylvia Plath and Anne Sexton, both of whom he taught at Harvard. They gave rise to the term 'confessional poetry', a term he hated but it has some accuracy. One critic described them as a form of ordered bleeding onto the page. *Life Studies* was followed in 1973 by the Pulitzer Prize-winning *The Dolphin*, which revealed, perhaps too brutally, the private pain of all concerned when Lowell (previously married to the short-story writer Jean Stafford) left his long marriage to the literary icon Elizabeth Hardwick for the stunningly beautiful, Booker Prize-winning novelist Caroline Blackwood, whom he subsequently married.

'(But our beginnings never know our ends)' is Eliot's chilling warning. Robert Lowell died of a heart attack in a taxi in New York in 1977. He was just sixty years old. He was carrying a brown paper parcel containing Lucien Freud's portrait of his then wife, Caroline Blackwood, which Grey (Lord) Gowrie, one-time chairman of Sotheby's, had procured for Lowell. It's a heartbreaking scene, and Lowell knew himself to be heartbreaking. He was right. He was also a great poet.

The Poems

'It's better to get your emotions out in a Macbeth than in a confession,' Lowell said in 1961, two years after *Life Studies*, which, he implied, would be his last autobiographical collection. And about that he was wrong. He had recreated himself in poetry once, in 1959, and though his life was to change dramatically when he left Elizabeth Hardwick and America (he became a visiting fellow at All Souls, Oxford, and a lecturer at Kent and Sussex) he would continue to carve out of the personal much of his most enduring poetry.

But not all. Lowell wrote two of the greatest political poems of this or any age, 'Waking Early Sunday Morning' and 'For the Union Dead' – title poem of his hugely praised 1964 collection. This last is a haunting tribute to Col. Robert Gould Shaw, white, twenty-five when he bravely led his Black 54 Massachusetts Regiment against Fort Wagner in the Civil War ('They relinquish everything to serve the Republic'). A monument to his courage by Augustus Saint-Gaudens stands in stark contrast to what Lowell perceives as a less honourable time. Lowell felt in his public utterances and behaviour the weight of history inherent in his family name. During anti-Vietnam demonstrations he had 'the unwilling haunted saintliness of a man who was repaying the moral debts of tens of generations of ancestors'. Norman Mailer at his most restrained. 'Commander Lowell', the poet's father – 'once / nineteen, the youngest ensign in his class, / he was "the old man" of a gunboat on the Yangtze' – is 'paid out' for his failure, more economic than moral in this brutal, minor masterpiece. In 'Memories of West Street and Lepke', written in the 'tranquillized *Fifties*, / and I am forty . . .', Lowell remembers his 'manic statement, / telling off the state and president' which led him to prison and to Lepke of Murder, Inc., 'the electric chair— / hanging like an oasis in his air / of lost connections . . .'

A perfect last line, and last lines, as Donne reminds us, 'are the stamp' that authenticates great poetry.

Perhaps his most unforgettable line lies just off-centre of one of his best poems, 'Skunk Hour' – his tribute to his great friend, the poet Elizabeth Bishop. It abruptly changes the rhythm of the poem, and stuns with its awful simplicity: 'My mind's not right.' 'Waking in the Blue' is a dazed love poem from McLean (psychiatric) Hospital as alumni of Boston University ponder I. A. Richard's *The Meaning of Meaning* with those who in their *jeunesse dorée* had been members of Harvard's exclusive club, Porcellian '29. Legend has it that if you did not make your first million by the time you were forty the club would give it to you! Now each holds 'a locked razor'.

The very handsome Lowell married three brilliant writers and was exquisitely sensitive to marital manoeuvres – even in the dark. In 'Man and Wife', her back now turned to him, her 'old-fashioned tirade— / loving, rapid, merciless— / breaks like the Atlantic Ocean on my head.' A line to be treasured. The poem is, according to one critic, in balance with the savage sexuality in '"To Speak of Woe That Is in Marriage"', as the female narrator bemoans 'the monotonous meanness of his lust'. Lowell said the poem owed a debt to Catullus. The imagery, however, of the woman who each night tapes a ten-dollar note and the man's car keys to her thigh is based on a shared insight from a friend into his clearly less than ecstatic marriage.

'I enjoyed writing about my life more than living it', Lowell said towards the end. 'Alas, I can only tell my own story.' His last poem, 'Epilogue', tells us again what it is he tried to do and at such cost. 'Yet why not say what happened? / Pray for the grace of accuracy . . . We are poor passing facts, / warned by that to give / each figure in the photograph / his living name.'

Commander Lowell

(1887–1950)

There were no undesirables or girls in my set,
when I was a boy at Mattapoisett—
only Mother, still her Father's daughter.
Her voice was still electric
with a hysterical, unmarried panic,
when she read to me from the Napoleon book.
Long-nosed Marie Louise
Hapsburg in the frontispiece
had a downright Boston bashfulness,
where she grovelled to Bonaparte, who scratched his navel,
and bolted his food—just my seven years tall!
And I, bristling and manic,
skulked in the attic,
and got two hundred French generals by name,
from A to V— from Augereau to Vandamme.
I used to dope myself asleep,
naming those unpronounceables like sheep.

Having a naval officer
for my Father was nothing to shout
about to the summer colony at 'Matt.'
He wasn't at all 'serious,'
when he showed up on the golf course,
wearing a blue serge jacket and numbly cut
white ducks he'd bought
at a Pearl Harbor commissariat . . .
and took four shots with his putter to sink his putt.

'Bob,' they said, 'golf's a game you really ought to know how to
  play,
if you play at all.'
They wrote him off as 'naval,'
naturally supposed his sport was sailing.
Poor Father, his training was engineering!
Cheerful and cowed
among the seadogs at the Sunday yacht club,
he was never one of the crowd.

'Anchors aweigh,' Daddy boomed in his bathtub,
'Anchors aweigh,'
when Lever Brothers offered to pay
him double what the Navy paid.
I nagged for his dress sword with gold braid,
and cringed because Mother, new
caps on all her teeth, was born anew
at forty. With seamanlike celerity,
Father left the Navy,
and deeded Mother his property.

He was soon fired. Year after year,
he still hummed 'Anchors aweigh' in the tub—
whenever he left a job,
he bought a smarter car.
Father's last employer
was Scudder, Stevens and Clark, Investment Advisors,
himself his only client.
While Mother dragged to bed alone,
read Menninger,
and grew more and more suspicious,
he grew defiant.
Night after night,
à la clarté déserte de sa lampe,
he slid his ivory Annapolis slide rule

across a pad of graphs—
piker speculations! In three years
he squandered sixty thousand dollars.

Smiling on all,
Father was once successful enough to be lost
in the mob of ruling-class Bostonians.
As early as 1928,
he owned a house converted to oil,
and redecorated by the architect
of St. Mark's School . . . Its main effect
was a drawing room, 'longitudinal as Versailles,'
its ceiling, roughened with oatmeal, was blue as the sea.
And once
nineteen, the youngest ensign in his class,
he was 'the old man' of a gunboat on the Yangtze.

Memories of West Street and Lepke

Only teaching on Tuesdays, book-worming
in pajamas fresh from the washer each morning,
I hog a whole house on Boston's
'hardly passionate Marlborough Street,'
where even the man
scavenging filth in the back alley trash cans,
has two children, a beach wagon, a helpmate,
and is a 'young Republican.'
I have a nine months' daughter,
young enough to be my granddaughter.
Like the sun she rises in her flame-flamingo infants' wear.

These are the tranquillized *Fifties*,
and I am forty. Ought I to regret my seedtime?
I was a fire-breathing Catholic C.O.,
and made my manic statement,
telling off the state and president, and then
sat waiting sentence in the bull pen
beside a Negro boy with curlicues
of marijuana in his hair.

Given a year,
I walked on the roof of the West Street Jail, a short
enclosure like my school soccer court,
and saw the Hudson River once a day
through sooty clothesline entanglements
and bleaching khaki tenements.
Strolling, I yammered metaphysics with Abramowitz,

a jaundice-yellow ('it's really tan')
and fly-weight pacifist,
so vegetarian,
he wore rope shoes and preferred fallen fruit.
He tried to convert Bioff and Brown,
the Hollywood pimps, to his diet.
Hairy, muscular, suburban,
wearing chocolate double-breasted suits,
they blew their tops and beat him black and blue.

I was so out of things, I'd never heard
of the Jehovah's Witnesses.
'Are you a C.O.?' I asked a fellow jailbird.
'No,' he answered, 'I'm a J.W.'
He taught me the 'hospital tuck,'
and pointed out the T-shirted back
of *Murder Incorporated*'s Czar Lepke,
there piling towels on a rack,
or dawdling off to his little segregated cell full
of things forbidden the common man:
a portable radio, a dresser, two toy American
flags tied together with a ribbon of Easter palm.
Flabby, bald, lobotomized,
he drifted in a sheepish calm,
where no agonizing reappraisal
jarred his concentration on the electric chair—
hanging like an oasis in his air
of lost connections. . . .

Skunk Hour

(For Elizabeth Bishop)

Nautilus Island's hermit
heiress still lives through winter in her Spartan cottage;
her sheep still graze above the sea.
Her son's a bishop. Her farmer
is first selectman in our village;
she's in her dotage.

Thirsting for
the hierarchic privacy
of Queen Victoria's century,
she buys up all
the eyesores facing her shore,
and lets them fall.

The season's ill—
we've lost our summer millionaire,
who seemed to leap from an L. L. Bean
catalogue. His nine-knot yawl
was auctioned off to lobstermen.
A red fox stain covers Blue Hill.

And now our fairy
decorator brightens his shop for fall;
his fishnet's filled with orange cork,
orange, his cobbler's bench and awl;
there is no money in his work,
he'd rather marry.

One dark night,
my Tudor Ford climbed the hill's skull;
I watched for love-cars. Lights turned down,
they lay together, hull to hull,
where the graveyard shelves on the town . . .
My mind's not right.

A car radio bleats,
'Love, O careless Love . . .' I hear
my ill-spirit sob in each blood cell,
as if my hand were at its throat. . . .
I myself am hell;
nobody's here—

only skunks, that search
in the moonlight for a bite to eat.
They march on their soles up Main Street:
white stripes, moonstruck eyes' red fire
under the chalk-dry and spar spire
of the Trinitarian Church.

I stand on top
of our back steps and breathe the rich air—
a mother skunk with her column of kittens swills the garbage pail.
She jabs her wedge-head in a cup
of sour cream, drops her ostrich tail,
and will not scare.

Waking in the Blue

The night attendant, a B.U. sophomore,
rouses from the mare's-nest of his drowsy head
propped on *The Meaning of Meaning*.
He catwalks down our corridor.
Azure day
makes my agonized blue window bleaker.
Crows maunder on the petrified fairway.
Absence! My heart grows tense
as though a harpoon were sparring for the kill.
(This is the house for the 'mentally ill.')

What use is my sense of humor?
I grin at Stanley, now sunk in his sixties,
once a Harvard all-American fullback,
(if such were possible!)
still hoarding the build of a boy in his twenties,
as he soaks, a ramrod
with the muscle of a seal
in his long tub,
vaguely urinous from the Victorian plumbing.
A kingly granite profile in a crimson golf-cap,
worn all day, all night,
he thinks only of his figure,
of slimming on sherbet and ginger ale—
more cut off from words than a seal.

This is the way day breaks in Bowditch Hall at McLean's;
the hooded night lights bring out 'Bobbie,'

Porcellian '29,
a replica of Louis XVI
without the wig—
redolent and roly-poly as a sperm whale,
as he swashbuckles about in his birthday suit
and horses at chairs.
These victorious figures of bravado ossified young.

In between the limits of day,
hours and hours go by under the crew haircuts
and slightly too little nonsensical bachelor twinkle
of the Roman Catholic attendants.
(There are no Mayflower
screwballs in the Catholic Church.)

After a hearty New England breakfast,
I weigh two hundred pounds
this morning. Cock of the walk,
I strut in my turtle-necked French sailor's jersey
before the metal shaving mirrors,
and see the shaky future grow familiar
in the pinched, indigenous faces
of these thoroughbred mental cases,
twice my age and half my weight.
We are all old-timers,
each of us holds a locked razor.

For the Union Dead

'Relinquunt Omnia Servare Rem Publicam.'

The old South Boston Aquarium stands
in a Sahara of snow now. Its broken windows are boarded.
The bronze weathervane cod has lost half its scales.
The airy tanks are dry.

Once my nose crawled like a snail on the glass;
my hand tingled
to burst the bubbles
drifting from the noses of the cowed, compliant fish.

My hand draws back. I often sigh still
for the dark downward and vegetating kingdom
of the fish and reptile. One morning last March
I pressed against the new barbed and galvanized

fence on the Boston Common. Behind their cage,
yellow dinosaur steamshovels were grunting
as they cropped up tons of mush and grass
to gouge their underworld garage.

Parking spaces luxuriate like civic
sandpiles in the heart of Boston.
A girdle of orange, Puritan-pumpkin colored girders
braces the tingling Statehouse,

shaking over the excavations, as it faces Colonel Shaw
and his bell-cheeked Negro infantry

on St. Gaudens' shaking Civil War relief,
propped by a plank splint against the garage's earthquake.

Two months after marching through Boston,
half the regiment was dead;
at the dedication,
William James could almost hear the bronze Negroes breathe.

Their monument sticks like a fishbone
in the city's throat.
Its Colonel is as lean
as a compass-needle.

He has an angry wrenlike vigilance,
a greyhound's gentle tautness;
he seems to wince at pleasure,
and suffocate for privacy.

He is out of bounds now. He rejoices in man's lovely,
peculiar power to choose life and die—
when he leads his black soldiers to death,
he cannot bend his back.

On a thousand small town New England greens,
the old white churches hold their air
of sparse, sincere rebellion; frayed flags
quilt the graveyards of the Grand Army of the Republic.

The stone statues of the abstract Union Soldier
grow slimmer and younger each year—
wasp-waisted, they doze over muskets
and muse through their sideburns . . .

Shaw's father wanted no monument
except the ditch,

where his son's body was thrown
and lost with his 'niggers.'

The ditch is nearer.
There are no statues for the last war here;
on Boylston Street, a commercial photograph
shows Hiroshima boiling

over a Mosler Safe, the 'Rock of Ages'
that survived the blast. Space is nearer.
When I crouch to my television set,
the drained faces of Negro school-children rise like balloons.

Colonel Shaw
is riding on his bubble,
he waits
for the blessèd break.

The Aquarium is gone. Everywhere,
giant finned cars nose forward like fish;
a savage servility
slides by on grease.

'To Speak of Woe That Is in Marriage'

'It is the future generation that presses into being by means of these
exuberant feelings and super-sensible soap bubbles of ours.'

SCHOPENHAUER

The hot night makes us keep our bedroom windows open.
Our magnolia blossoms. Life begins to happen.
My hopped up husband drops his home disputes,
and hits the streets to cruise for prostitutes,
free-lancing out along the razor's edge.
This screwball might kill his wife, then take the pledge.
Oh the monotonous meanness of his lust . . .
It's the injustice . . . he is so unjust—
whiskey-blind, swaggering home at five.
My only thought is how to keep alive.
What makes him tick? Each night now I tie
ten dollars and his car key to my thigh. . . .
Gored by the climacteric of his want,
he stalls above me like an elephant.'

Man and Wife

Tamed by *Miltown*, we lie on Mother's bed;
the rising sun in war paint dyes us red;
in broad daylight her gilded bed-posts shine,
abandoned, almost Dionysian.
At last the trees are green on Marlborough Street,
blossoms on our magnolia ignite
the morning with their murderous five days' white.
All night I've held your hand,
as if you had
a fourth time faced the kingdom of the mad—
its hackneyed speech, its homicidal eye—
and dragged me home alive. . . . Oh my *Petite*,
clearest of all God's creatures, still all air and nerve:
you were in your twenties, and I,
once hand on glass
and heart in mouth,
outdrank the Rahvs in the heat
of Greenwich Village, fainting at your feet—
too boiled and shy
and poker-faced to make a pass,
while the shrill verve
of your invective scorched the traditional South.

Now twelve years later, you turn your back.
Sleepless, you hold
your pillow to your hollows like a child;
your old-fashioned tirade—
loving, rapid, merciless—
breaks like the Atlantic Ocean on my head.

Epilogue

Those blessèd structures, plot and rhyme—
why are they no help to me now
I want to make
something imagined, not recalled?
I hear the noise of my own voice:
The painter's vision is not a lens,
it trembles to caress the light.
But sometimes everything I write
with the threadbare art of my eye
seems a snapshot,
lurid, rapid, garish, grouped,
heightened from life,
yet paralyzed by fact.
All's misalliance.
Yet why not say what happened?
Pray for the grace of accuracy
Vermeer gave to the sun's illumination
stealing like the tide across a map
to his girl solid with yearning.
We are poor passing facts,
warned by that to give
each figure in the photograph
his living name.

JOHN MILTON

John Milton was born in London in 1608. A poet, political philosopher and pamphleteer, his life was dedicated for over twenty years to the cause of republicanism. His masterpiece *Paradise Lost* was not completed until 1663, by which time he was totally blind. It was followed by *Paradise Regained* (1671) and *Samson Agonistes* – possibly in the same year. He is the greatest epic poet in the English language. He died in 1674.

JOHN MILTON

Simply Sublime

A young John Milton, to his schoolfriend Charles Diodata: 'Allow me to use big language with you. You ask what I am thinking of? I am thinking of immortality. What am I doing? Growing my wings and meditating flight. But as yet our Pegasus raises himself on very tender wings. Let us be lowly wise.'

This charming image, the seductive humility of the last lines, cannot disguise the towering nature of the ambition – immortality. *Paradise Lost*, published when Milton was sixty, 'long choosing and beginning late', fulfilled his desire 'to leave something so written to after times as they should not willingly let it die'. We haven't, and 'after times' won't. The poem, over ten thousand words long, bestowed on Milton a form of poetic deity. He is variously described as divine (Wordsworth), sublime (Byron), and, for Coleridge, 'Milton is the deity of prescience'. Ted Hughes believed there is 'a direct line which can be traced from Virgil to Dante, from Dante to Milton'. (It continued, Hughes noted, to Eliot.)

Milton on Mount Parnassus. How did he get there? John Milton was born on 9 December 1608 in Bread Street in London's Cheapside to John Milton Snr, a wealthy scrivener and an excellent composer of music, whose own father, the keeper of the Forest of Shotover and a zealous papist, disinherited his son because he'd forsaken the religion of his ancestors. Disobedience in pursuit of intellectual and spiritual freedom requires courage. Milton learnt early that courage comes at a cost, though in the light of his father's success he may also have deduced it was not necessarily prohibitive. Initially he was educated at home, then at St Paul's School, followed by Christ's College, Cambridge, where, perhaps due to his good looks (he had wonderful hair) he was known as Our Lady of Christs. His 'honest haughtiness' (his phrase) did not endear him either to his fellow students or to teachers and, according to Dr Johnson, Milton, who may have been rusticated, was possibly one of the last students to suffer the indignity of 'corporal correction'. At Cambridge he wrote the oft-anthologised 'Il Pensoroso', the contemplative man who praises Melancholy, and its companion piece, 'L'Allegro', in which Melancholy is banished in favour of the delightful invitation to 'come, and trip it as ye go / on the light fantastic toe'. Seduction by argument drives his Mask, the rather strange *Comus*, rarely performed (perhaps advisedly), in which 'The Lady' is implored by Comus to 'be not cosen'd with that same vaunted name Virginity . . . if you let slip time, like a neglected rose / It withers on the stalk with languish'd head . . . Beauty is nature's brag.' In 'Lycidas', his haunting monody (written in memory of Edward King, a college contemporary drowned in the Irish Sea), pastoral beauty is in disturbing contrast to violent images of the drowning young man's futile battle with the sea. The philosopher's instinct to set in balance opposing views is clear in these early poems. They are a powerful harbinger of things to come – later, much later, after decades of political dissent and of little poetry.

Milton initially rejected a life in the Church – 'a clergyman must subscribe slave . . . bought and begun with servitude and forswearing', which was not his style . . . 'Thoughts of Obedience, whether Canonical or Civil, raised his indignation', said Dr Johnson. Instead he dedicated himself to six years' intense study of Greek, Latin and Hebrew (Milton is perhaps literature's most erudite poet). He then embarked on a tour of Europe, where he visited Galileo – no doubt a perfect meeting of minds – though we have no record of the conversation. In 1639, aged thirty-one, he returned to England to what was about to become the most turbulent period in its history – the Civil War and the execution of a king. The ardent Platonist had found the cause of his life, Republicanism; it would cost him dearly. Starting in

1641 Milton's life and his brilliance were to be dedicated to a tireless, personally dangerous series of writings in defence of liberty, be it religious or civil – the philosophical cornerstone of his masterpiece should he live long enough to write it. Macaulay spoke of the 'deadly hatred which he bore to bigots and tyrants' and of 'the faith which he so sternly kept with his country'. From 1641 almost twenty years passed of passionate politics, philosophy, marriages, births and deaths, during which Milton would serve as Secretary of Foreign Tongues under Oliver Cromwell and write, with reckless courage, two months after the execution of Charles I, 'The Tenure of Kings and Magistrates'. An ardent pamphleteer, he published attacks on the episcopacy, particularly Bishops Usher and Hall: 'Of Reformation in England and the Causes that Hitherto Have Hindered It'; and on the Government in the still-stirring 'Areopagitica' – his great defence of the liberty of the press and the only work by a poet to have legal stature in American courts. According to Professor Myron Taylor the Bill of Rights owes more to John Milton than to John Locke. His work would be publicly burnt in Europe.

Private life was hardly much calmer. His first wife left him after six weeks of marriage, thus inspiring his pamphlet on divorce, 'The Doctrine and Discipline of Divorce'. She returned, perhaps influenced by the pamphlet or, possibly, the fact that he'd courted 'a young lady of great accomplishments', a certain Miss Davis. Milton married three times; death, rather than divorce, was the catalyst. These marriages produced a son, who died, and three daughters. Though Dr Johnson commented rather meanly that on the death of his second wife, Katherine Woodcock (who died after fifteen months of marriage, aged just thirty), 'the poet honoured her memory with a poor sonnet', the poem is very lovely indeed. Milton, dreaming of his dead wife, cries out, 'But O as to embrace me she enclined, / I wak'd, she fled, and day brought back my night.'

There was another, more terrible darkness which would engulf him – blindness. By 1651 Milton, aged only forty-three, was totally blind. 'The most important fact about Milton for my purpose is his blindness . . . it would seem indeed to have helped him concentrate on what he could do best,' wrote Eliot. Stripped of all political involvement by the Restoration in 1660, blind and battered, arrested and released (Marvell was one of those who pleaded for him), Milton, forced to 'stand and wait' – didn't. He was, according to Harold Bloom, 'unsinkable, there may be no larger triumph of the visionary will in western literature'. *Paradise Lost*, published 27 April 1667, was followed in 1671 by *Paradise Regained*.

Milton died on 8 November 1674, a month before his sixty-sixth birthday. One hopes he died 'calm of mind, all passion spent', the last line of his final great poem, *Samson Agonistes*.

Paradise Lost

It's a long poem. 'No man ever wished *Paradise Lost* were longer', according to Dr Johnson. However, to 'justify the ways of God to men' is no mean task. God, as we all know, moves in mysterious ways. In *Paradise Lost*, Milton's God, as William Empson tells us, can be mysteriously repellent: 'God started all the trouble in the first place . . . the reason why the poem is so good is that it makes God so bad.' It is also the reason it is so thrilling. God, as Shelley noted, is alleged to have no moral superiority over his adversary, Satan. The sheer moral courage that this required of the 'central Protestant poet' is sublime. Milton's psychological insights into the soul of Satan, tortured by Freudian ambivalence, loving and hating God at the same time, makes Satan one the most enduringly tragic figures in all literature. Rage at rejection and displacement fuels his rebellion and his destruction. God, without warning, announces to all Heaven 'This day I have begot whom I declare / My onely Son, and on this holy Hill / Him have anointed, whom ye now behold / At my right hand; Your head I him appoint; / And by my Self have sworn to him shall bow / All knees in Heav'n, and shall confess him Lord.' And that's an order! The penalty for disobedience? Severe. 'Him who disobeys' will be 'cast out from God . . . into utter darkness . . . his place ordained without redemption.' Satan, previously known as Lucifer, bringer of light, fights back magnificently. He has a cause. We will be sacrificed to it. For eternity. The stakes, as they say, are high. Satan works on a grander scale than Iago, to whom he is sometimes compared, 'bringing down all mankind rather than one brave but limited general': Harold Bloom at his most succinct.

Initially, *Paradise Lost* was planned as a drama, a stage tragedy in five acts entitled *Adam Unparadised*. Why did Milton change his mind? Shakespeare, Bloom suggests, was the catalyst. Milton, who was seven when Shakespeare died, knew the eternal genius of Shakespeare's plays could never be surpassed, and perhaps an example of Bloom's 'anxiety of influence' can be seen at work in Milton, who from youth longed for immortality. So he struck out in another direction, the Epic Poem. However, he would write it in blank verse, previously confined to the drama, 'rhyme being no necessary adjunct or true ornament of poem or good verse'. A decision of genius. Milton is, as Eliot noted, 'outside the theatre our greatest master of freedom within form'. Though Eliot feared the weight of Milton's language had a deadening effect, as did Addison, he also acknowledged in his essay 'Milton II' that 'the full beauty of the line is found in its context – and that is conclusive evidence of his supreme mastery'.

Within the line and form of his epic masterpiece lies literature's most passionate intellectual argument for freedom of will, a passion grounded in a lifetime's courageous dedication to its cause, in language of beauty and logic and wisdom – the triumph of the man blind and ill, and of the poet. In the face of his achievement we stand astonished. How did he do it? In his head. Sometimes, in the middle of the night, Milton, suddenly inspired, called to his daughters to 'secure what came' – and thereby hangs a tale. No doubt he was a difficult man and in extreme difficulty. His gift to us was *Paradise Lost*.

Milton must be read aloud, according to Douglas Bush. The passages we have selected from Book I (lines 105–24; 249–63) are from Satan's speech as he rallies his fallen angels burning in Hell. It is a hymn to courage, to independence: 'The mind is its own place, and in itself / Can make a Heav'n of Hell, a Hell of Heav'n . . . Better to reign in Hell, than serve in Heav'n.' It is little wonder Blake wrote of Milton that 'he was a true Poet and of the Devil's party without knowing it'. In the selection from Book IX Satan, now in the guise of snake in the Garden of Eden, has resolved that 'all good to me is lost; / Evil, be thou my good. . . .' and plots the downfall of Adam and Eve, whom he overhears in a (celestial) argument about – what else? – freedom. Eve wishes to be free to wander alone in the garden, Adam the anxious first man is worried but surrenders to Eve – *plus ça change.* Eve encounters Satan, who appeals not only to her vanity but also to something more noble – her desire for Knowledge, which resides in the Tree of Knowledge, the only tree in the Garden of Eden forbidden to Adam and Eve. God at his most perverse. A fearful Eve is reassured by Satan: 'ye shall not die: How should ye? by the fruit? it gives you life / To knowledge.' Eve succumbs, and having eaten of the fruit she muses on the power of Knowledge – and in contemplating the first female lie she wonders whether she really ought to keep the Knowledge, i.e. the power, to herself . . . and be the superior one. On the other hand if the warning is right she will die and comes there another Eve? 'Adam wedded to another Eve, / Shall live with her enjoying, I extinct;', a less than pleasing prospect to our first mother. Therefore Adam too must eat of the tree. If she's doomed, he's coming with her – a rather searing insight into female psychology. She now sets out to persuade as she has been persuaded. She understands her man. For Adam, knowing immediately Eve is doomed, sacrifices himself for love: 'flesh of flesh / Bone of my bone thou art, and from thy state / Mine never shall be parted, bliss or woe'. He eats the fruit and is immediately enflamed by carnal desire to which Eve delightedly responds and, as Milton tells us, with considerable erotic power: 'in lust they burn'. Off they go, our first parents, to a shady bank in the garden and to the inevitable. Just as inevitably, the first act of intercourse results in the first post-coital guilt followed, alas, by the first post-coital blame game – If only you had listened to me etc. – and we part from this short excerpt in the midst of a male–female battle which, like *Paradise Lost*, will continue for eternity.

Thousands of glorious lines later our sad banished parents are led by 'the hast'ning Angel' from Paradise. 'Some natural tears they dropp'd, but wip'd them soon'. All, it would seem, is not lost. Milton's strangely healing last lines tell us 'The World was all before them, where to choose / Their place of rest, and Providence their guide: / They hand in hand, with wand'ring steps and slow, / Through *Eden* took their solitary way.'

The End. And the beginning . . .

Paradise Lost

[excerpts]

from Book I

> What though the field be lost?
> All is not lost; the unconquerable will,
> And study of revenge, immortal hate,
> And courage never to submit or yield:
> And what is else not to be overcome?
> That glory never shall his wrath or might
> Extort from me. To bow and sue for grace
> With suppliant knee, and deify his power
> Who from the terror of this arm so late
> Doubted his empire, that were low indeed,
> That were an ignominy and shame beneath
> This downfall; since by Fate the strength of gods
> And this empyreal substance cannot fail,
> Since through experience of this great event
> In arms not worse, in foresight much advanced,
> We may with more successful hope resolve
> To wage by force or guile eternal war
> Irreconcilable, to our grand Foe,
> Who now triúmphs, and in th' excess of joy
> Sole reigning holds the tyranny of Heav'n.

> . . .

> Farewell happy fields
> Where joy for ever dwells: hail horrors, hail
> Infernal world, and thou profoundest Hell
> Receive thy new possessor: one who brings
> A mind not to be changed by place or time.

The mind is its own place, and in itself
Can make a Heav'n of Hell, a Hell of Heav'n.
What matter where, if I be still the same,
And what I should be, all but less than he
Whom thunder hath made greater? Here at least
We shall be free; th' Almighty hath not built
Here for his envy, will not drive us hence:
Here we may reign secure, and in my choice
To reign is worth ambition though in Hell:
Better to reign in Hell, than serve in Heav'n.

from Book IV [Satan is in soliloquy]

Ah gentle pair, ye little think how nigh
Your change approaches, when all these delights
Will vanish and deliver ye to woe,
More woe, the more your taste is now of joy;
Happy, but for so happy ill secured
Long to continue, and this high seat your Heav'n
Ill fenced for Heav'n to keep out such a foe
As now is entered; yet no purposed foe
To you whom I could pity thus forlorn
Though I unpitied: league with you I seek,
And mutual amity so strait, so close,
That I with you must dwell, or you with me
Henceforth

from Book IX [Adam and Eve are in dialogue]

Daughter of God and man, immortal Eve,
For such thou art, from sin and blame entire:
Not diffident of thee do I dissuade
Thy absence from my sight, but to avoid
Th' attempt itself, intended by our Foe.

For he who tempts, though in vain, at least asperses
The tempted with dishonour foul, supposed
Not incorruptible of faith, not proof
Against temptation: thou thyself with scorn
And anger wouldst resent the offered wrong,
Though ineffectual found: misdeem not then,
If such affront I labour to avert
From thee alone, which on us both at once
The Enemy, though bold, will hardly dare,
Or daring, first on me th' assault shall light.
Nor thou his malice and false guile contemn;
Subtle he needs must be, who could seduce
Angels, nor think superfluous others' aid.
I from the influence of thy looks receive
Accéss in every virtue, in thy sight
More wise, more watchful, stronger, if need were
Of outward strength; while shame, thou looking on,
Shame to be overcome or overreached
Would utmost vigour raise, and raised unite.
Why shouldst not thou like sense within thee feel
When I am present, and thy trial choose
With me, best witness of thy virtue tried.
　　So spake domestic Adam in his care
And matrimonial love; but Eve, who thought
Less attributed to her faith sincere,
Thus her reply with accent sweet renewed.
　　If this be our condition, thus to dwell
In narrow circuit straitened by a Foe,
Subtle or violent, we not endued
Single with like defence, wherever met,
How are we happy, still in fear of harm?
But harm precedes not sin: only our Foe
Tempting affronts us with his foul esteem
Of our integrity: his foul esteem

Sticks no dishonour on our front, but turns
Foul on himself; then wherefore shunned or feared
By us? Who rather double honour gain
From his surmise proved false, find peace within,
Favour from Heav'n, our witness from th' event.
And what is faith, love, virtue unassayed
Alone, without exterior help sustained?
Let us not then suspect our happy state
Left so imperfect by the Maker wise,
As not secure to single or combined.
Frail is our happiness, if this be so,
And Eden were no Eden thus exposed.
　　To whom thus Adam fervently replied.
O woman, best are all things as the will
Of God ordained them; his creating hand
Nothing imperfect or deficient left
Of all that he created, much less man,
Or aught that might his happy state secure,
Secure from outward force; within himself
The danger lies, yet lies within his power:
Against his will he can receive no harm.
But God left free the will, for what obeys
Reason, is free, and reason he made right,
But bid her well beware, and still erect,
Lest by some fair appearing good surprised
She dictate false, and misinform the will
To do what God expressly hath forbid.
Not then mistrust, but tender love enjoins,
That I should mind thee oft, and mind thou me.
Firm we subsist, yet possible to swerve,
Since reason not impossibly may meet
Some specious object by the Foe suborned,
And fall into deception unaware,
Not keeping strictest watch, as she was warned.
Seek not temptation then, which to avoid

Were better, and most likely if from me
Thou sever not: trial will come unsought.
Wouldst thou approve thy constancy, approve
First thy obedience; th' other who can know,
Not seeing thee attempted, who attest?
But if thou think, trial unsought may find
Us both securer than thus warned thou seem'st,
Go; for thy stay, not free, absents thee more;
Go in thy native innocence, rely
On what thou hast of virtue, summon all,
For God towards thee hath done his part, do thine.

      . . .

[Eve] from her husband's hand her hand
Soft she withdrew

      . . .

O much deceived, much failing, hapless Eve,
Of thy presumed return! event perverse!
Thou never from that hour in Paradise
Found'st either sweet repast, or sound repose;
Such ambush hid among sweet flow'rs and shades
Waited with Hellish rancour imminent
To intercept thy way, or send thee back
Despoiled of innocence, of faith, of bliss.
For now, and since first break of dawn the Fiend,
Mere serpent in appearance, forth was come,
And on his quest, where likeliest he might find
The only two of mankind, but in them
The whole included race, his purposed prey.
In bow'r and field he sought, where any tuft
Of grove or garden-plot more pleasant lay,
Their tendance or plantation for delight;
By fountain or by shady rivulet
He sought them both, but wished his hap might find

Eve separate; he wished, but not with hope
Of what so seldom chanced, when to his wish,
Beyond his hope, Eve separate he spies

. . .

Thoughts, whither have ye led me, with what sweet
Compulsion thus transported to forget
What hither brought us, hate, not love, nor hope
Of Paradise for Hell, hope here to taste
Of pleasure, but all pleasure to destroy,
Save what is in destroying; other joy
To me is lost. Then let me not let pass
Occasion which now smiles; behold alone
The woman, opportune to all attempts,
Her husband, for I view far round, not nigh,
Whose higher intellectual more I shun,
And strength, of courage haughty, and of limb
Heroic built, though of terrestrial mould,
Foe not informidable, exempt from wound,
I not; so much hath Hell debased, and pain
Enfeebled me, to what I was in Heav'n.
She fair, divinely fair, fit love for gods,
Not terrible, though terror be in love
And beauty, not approached by stronger hate,
Hate stronger, under show of love well-feigned,
The way which to her ruin now I tend.

. . .

Into the heart of Eve his words made way

. . .

Empress, the way is ready, and not long,
Beyond a row of myrtles, on a flat,
Fast by a fountain, one small thicket past
Of blowing myrrh and balm; if thou accept

My conduct, I can bring thee thither soon.
　　Lead then, said Eve. He leading swiftly rolled
In tangles, and made intricate seem straight,
To mischief swift.

　　　. . .

So glistered the dire snake, and into fraud
Led Eve our credulous mother, to the tree
Of prohibition, root of all our woe;
which when she saw, thus to her guide she spake.
　　Serpent, we might have spared our coming hither,
Fruitless to me, though fruit be here to excess,
The credit of whose virtue rest with thee,
Wondrous indeed, if cause of such effects.
But of this tree we may not taste nor touch;
God so commanded, and left that command
Sole daughter of his voice; the rest, we live
Law to ourselves, our reason is our law.
　　To whom the Tempter guilefully replied.
Indeed? hath God then said that of the fruit
Of all these garden trees ye shall not eat,
Yet lords declared of all in earth or air?
To whom thus Eve yet sinless. Of the fruit
Of each tree in the garden we may eat,
But of the fruit of this fair tree amidst
The garden, God hath said, Ye shall not eat
Thereof, nor shall ye touch it, lest ye die.

　　　. . .

Queen of this universe, do not believe
Those rigid threats of death; ye shall not die:
How should ye? by the fruit? it gives you life
To knowledge. By the Threat'ner? look on me,
Me who have touched and tasted, yet both live,
And life more perfect have attained than Fate

Meant me, by vent'ring higher than my lot.
Shall that be shut to man, which to the beast
Is open? or will God incense his ire
For such a petty trespass, and not praise
Rather your dauntless virtue, whom the pain
Of death denounced, whatever thing death be,
Deterred not from achieving what might lead
To happier life, knowledge of good and evil;

    . . .

And what are gods that man may not become
As they, participating god-like food?
The gods are first, and that advantage use
On our belief, that all from them proceeds;
I question it, for this fair earth I see,
Warmed by the sun, producing every kind,
Them nothing: if they all things, who enclosed
Knowledge of good and evil in this tree,
That whoso eats thereof, forthwith attains
Wisdom without their leave? and wherein lies
Th' offence, that man should thus attain to know?
What can your knowledge hurt him, or this tree
Impart against his will if all be his?
Or is it envy, and can envy dwell
In Heav'nly breasts? these, these and many more
Causes import your need of this fair fruit.
Goddess humane, reach then, and freely taste.

    . . .

[Eve is in soliloquy]

Here grows the cure of all, this fruit divine,
Fair to the eye, inviting to the taste,
Of virtue to make wise: what hinders then
To reach, and feed at once both body and mind?

So saying, her rash hand in evil hour
Forth reaching to the fruit, she plucked, she ate:
Earth felt the wound, and Nature from her seat
Sighing through all her works gave signs of woe,
That all was lost. Back to the thicket slunk
The guilty serpent, and well might, for Eve
Intent now wholly on her taste, naught else
Regarded, such delight till then, as seemed,
In fruit she never tasted, whether true
Or fancied so, through expectation high
Of knowledge, nor was Godhead from her thought.
Greedily she engorged without restraint,
And knew not eating death: satiate at length,
And heightened as with wine, jocund and boon,
Thus to herself she pleasingly began.

　　　. . .

　　　　I grow mature
In knowledge, as the gods who all things know;
Though others envy what they cannot give;

　　　. . .

　　　　　But to Adam in what sort
Shall I appear? shall I to him make known
As yet my change, and give him to partake
Full happiness with me, or rather not,
But keep the odds of knowledge in my power
Without copartner? so to add what wants
In female sex, the more to draw his love,
And render me more equal, and perhaps,
A thing not undesirable, sometime
Superior; for inferior who is free?
This may be well: but what if God have seen,
And death ensue? then I shall be no more,
And Adam wedded to another Eve,

Shall live with her enjoying, I extinct;
A death to think. Confirmed then I resolve,
Adam shall share with me in bliss or woe:
So dear I love him, that with him all deaths
I could endure, without him live no life.

. . .

Adam the while
Waiting desirous her return, had wove
Of choicest flow'rs a garland to adorn
Her tresses, and her rural labours crown,
As reapers oft are wont their harvest queen.
Great joy he promised to his thoughts, and new
Solace in her return, so long delayed;
Yet oft his heart, divine of something ill
Misgave him; he the falt'ring measure felt;
And forth to meet her went, the way she took
That morn when first they parted; by the Tree
Of Knowledge he must pass, there he her met,
Scarce from the tree returning; in her hand
A bough of fairest fruit that downy smiled,
New gathered, and ambrosial smell diffused.
To him she hasted, in her face excuse
Came prologue, and apology to prompt,
Which with bland words at will she thus addressed.
   Hast thou not wondered, Adam, at my stay?
Thee I have missed, and thought it long, deprived
Thy presence, agony of love till now
Not felt, nor shall be twice, for never more
Mean I to try, what rash untried I sought,
The pain of absence from thy sight. But strange
Hath been the cause, and wonderful to hear:
This tree is not as we are told, a tree
Of danger tasted, nor to evil unknown
Op'ning the way, but of divine effect

To open eyes, and make them gods who taste;
And hath been tasted such: the serpent wise,
Or not restrained as we, or not obeying,
Hath eaten of the fruit, and is become,
Not dead, as we are threatened, but thenceforth
Endued with human voice and human sense,
Reasoning to admiration, and with me
Persuasively hath so prevailed, that I
Have also tasted, and have also found
Th' effects to correspond, opener mine eyes,
Dim erst, dilated spirits, ampler heart,
And growing up to godhead; which for thee
Chiefly I sought, without thee can despise.
For bliss, as thou hast part, to me is bliss,
Tedious, unshared with thee, and odious soon.
Thou therefore also taste, that equal lot
May join us, equal joy, as equal love;
Lest thou not tasting, different degree
Disjoin us, and I then too late renounce
Deity for thee, when Fate will not permit.
    Thus Eve with count'nance blithe her story told;
But in her cheek distemper flushing glowed.
On th' other side, Adam, soon as he heard
The fatal trespass done by Eve, amazed,
Astonied stood and blank, while horror chill
Ran through his veins, and all his joints relaxed;
From his slack hand the garland wreathed for Eve
Down dropped, and all the faded roses shed:
Speechless he stood and pale, till thus at length
First to himself he inward silence broke.
    O fairest of Creation, last and best
Of all God's works, creature in whom excelled
Whatever can to sight or thought be formed,
Holy, divine, good, amiable or sweet!
How art thou lost, how on a sudden lost,

Defaced, deflow'red, and now to death devote?
Rather how hast thou yielded to transgress
The strict forbiddance, how to violate
The sacred fruit forbidd'n! Some cursèd fraud
Of Enemy hath beguiled thee, yet unknown,
And me with thee hath ruined, for with thee
Certain my resolution is to die;
How can I live without thee, how forgo
Thy sweet convérse and love so dearly joined,
To live again in these wild woods forlorn?
Should God create another Eve, and I
Another rib afford, yet loss of thee
Would never from my heart; no no, I feel
The link of nature draw me: flesh of flesh,
Bone of my bone thou art, and from thy state
Mine never shall be parted, bliss or woe.

So having said, as one from sad dismay
Recomforted, and after thoughts disturbed
Submitting to what seemed remédiless,
Thus in calm mood his words to Eve he turned.

Bold deed thou hast presumed, advent'rous Eve,
And peril great provoked, who thus hath dared
Had it been only coveting to eye
That sacred fruit, sacred to abstinence,
Much more to taste it under ban to touch.
But past who can recall, or done undo?
Not God omnipotent, nor Fate, yet so
Perhaps thou shalt not die, perhaps the fact
Is not so heinous now, foretasted fruit,
Profaned first by the serpent, by him first
Made common and unhallowed ere our taste;
Nor yet on him found deadly; he yet lives,
Lives, as thou saidst, and gains to live as man
Higher degree of life, inducement strong
To us, as likely tasting to attain

Proportional ascent, which cannot be
But to be gods, or angels demi-gods.
Nor can I think that God, Creator wise,
Though threat'ning, will in earnest so destroy
Us his prime creatures, dignified so high,
Set over all his works, which in our Fall,
For us created, needs with us must fail,
Dependent made; so God shall uncreate,
Be frustrate, do, undo, and labour lose,
Not well conceived of God, who though his power
Creation could repeat, yet would be loath
Us to abolish, lest the Adversary
Triúmph and say; Fickle their state whom God
Most favours, who can please him long? Me first
He ruined, now mankind; whom will he next?
Matter of scorn, not to be given the Foe.
However I with thee have fixed my lot,
Certain to undergo like doom; if death
Consort with thee, death is to me as life;
So forcible within my heart I feel
The bond of nature draw me to my own,
My own in thee, for what thou art is mine;
Our state cannot be severed, we are one,
One flesh; to lose thee were to lose myself.
　　So Adam, and thus Eve to him replied.
O glorious trial of exceeding love,
Illustrious evidence, example high!
Engaging me to emulate, but short
Of thy perfection, how shall I attain,
Adam, from whose dear side I boast me sprung,
And gladly of our union hear thee speak,
One heart, one soul in both; whereof good proof
This day affords, declaring thee resolved,
Rather than death or aught than death more dread
Shall separate us, linked in love so dear,

To undergo with me one guilt, one crime,
If any be, of tasting this fair fruit,
Whose virtue, for of good still good proceeds,
Direct, or by occasion hath presented
This happy trial of thy love, which else
So eminently never had been known.
Were it I thought death menaced would ensue
This my attempt, I would sustain alone
The worst, and not persuade thee, rather die
Deserted, than oblige thee with a fact
Pernicious to thy peace, chiefly assured
Remarkably so late of thy so true,
So faithful love unequalled; but I feel
Far otherwise th' event, not death, but life
Augmented, opened eyes, new hopes, new joys,
Taste so divine, that what of sweet before
Hath touched my sense, flat seems to this, and harsh.
On my experience, Adam, freely taste,
And fear of death deliver to the winds.

   So saying, she embraced him, and for joy
Tenderly wept, much won that he his love
Had so ennobled, as of choice to incur
Divine displeasure for her sake, or death.
In recompense (for such compliance bad
Such recompense best merits) from the bough
She gave him of that fair enticing fruit
With liberal hand: he scrupled not to eat
Against his better knowledge, not deceived,
But fondly overcome with female charm.
Earth trembled from her entrails, as again
In pangs, and Nature gave a second groan;
Sky loured, and muttering thunder, some sad drops
Wept at completing of the mortal sin
Original; while Adam took no thought,
Eating his fill, nor Eve to iterate

Her former trespass feared, the more to soothe
Him with her loved society, that now
As with new wine intoxicated both
They swim in mirth, and fancy that they feel
Divinity within them breeding wings
Wherewith to scorn the earth: but that false fruit
Far other operation first displayed,
Carnal desire inflaming; he on Eve
Began to cast lascivious eyes, she him
As wantonly repaid; in lust they burn:
Till Adam thus gan Eve to dalliance move.

   Eve, now I see thou art exact of taste,
And elegant, of sapience no small part,
Since to each meaning savour we apply,
And palate call judicious; I the praise
Yield thee, so well this day thou hast purveyed.
Much pleasure we have lost, while we abstained
From this delightful fruit, nor known till now
True relish, tasting; if such pleasure be
In things to us forbidden, it might be wished,
For this one tree had been forbidden ten.
But come, so well refreshed, now let us play,
As meet is, after such delicious fare;
For never did thy beauty since the day
I saw thee first and wedded thee, adorned
With all perfections, so inflame my sense
With ardour to enjoy thee, fairer now
Than ever, bounty of this virtuous tree.
   So said he, and forbore not glance or toy
Of amorous intent, well understood
Of Eve, whose eye darted contagious fire.
Her hand he seized, and to a shady bank,
Thick overhead with verdant roof embow'red
He led her nothing loath; flow'rs were the couch,
Pansies, and violets, and asphodel,

And hyacinth, earth's freshest softest lap.
There they their fill of love and love's disport
Took largely, of their mutual guilt the seal,
The solace of their sin, till dewy sleep
Oppressed them, wearied with their amorous play.
Soon as the force of that fallacious fruit,
That with exhilarating vapour bland
About their spirits had played, and inmost powers
Made err, was now exhaled, and grosser sleep
Bred of unkindly fumes, with conscious dreams
Encumbered, now had left them, up they rose
As from unrest, and each the other viewing,
Soon found their eyes how opened, and their minds
How darkened; innocence, that as a veil
Had shadowed them from knowing ill, was gone;
Just confidence, and native righteousness
And honour from about them, naked left
To guilty Shame: he covered, but his robe
Uncovered more. So rose the Danite strong
Hercúlean Samson from the harlot-lap
Of Phílistéan Dálila, and waked
Shorn of his strength, they destitute and bare
Of all their virtue: silent, and in face
Confounded long they sat, as strucken mute,
Till Adam, though not less than Eve abashed,
At length gave utterance to these words constrained.
    O Eve, in evil hour thou didst give ear
To that false worm, of whomsoever taught
To counterfeit man's voice, true in our Fall,
False in our promised rising; since our eyes
Opened we find indeed, and find we know
Both good and evil, good lost, and evil got,
Bad fruit of knowledge, if this be to know,
Which leaves us naked thus, of honour void,
Of innocence, of faith, of purity,

Our wonted ornaments now soiled and stained,
And in our faces evident the signs
Of foul concupiscence; whence evil store;
Even shame, the last of evils; of the first
Be sure then. How shall I behold the face
Henceforth of God or angel, erst with joy
And rapture so oft beheld? those Heav'nly shapes
Will dazzle now this earthly, with their blaze
Insufferably bright. O might I here
In solitude live savage, in some glade
Obscured, where highest woods impenetrable
To star or sunlight, spread their umbrage broad
And brown as evening: cover me ye pines,
Ye cedars, with innumerable boughs
Hide me, where I may never see them more.
But let us now, as in bad plight, devise
What best may for the present serve to hide
The parts of each from other, that seem most
To shame obnoxious, and unseemliest seen
Some tree whose broad smooth leaves together sewed,
And girded on our loins, may cover round
Those middle parts, that this new comer, Shame,
There sit not, and reproach us as unclean.
    So counselled he, and both together went
Into the thickest wood, there soon they chose
The fig-tree . . .
They gathered, broad as Amazonian targe,
And with what skill they had, together sewed,
To gird their waist, vain covering if to hide
Their guilt and dreaded shame; O how unlike
To that first naked glory. Such of late
Columbus found th' American so girt
With feathered cincture, naked else and wild
Among the trees on isles and woody shores.
Thus fenced, and as they thought, their shame in part

Covered, but not at rest or ease of mind,
They sat them down to weep, nor only tears
Rained at their eyes, but high winds worse within
Began to rise, high passions, anger, hate,
Mistrust, suspicion, discord, and shook sore
Their inward state of mind, calm region once
And full of peace, now tossed and turbulent:
For understanding ruled not, and the will
Heard not her lore, both in subjection now
To sensual appetite, who from beneath
Usurping over sov'reign reason claimed
Superior sway: from thus distempered breast,
Adam, estranged in look and altered style,
Speech intermitted thus to Eve renewed.

 Would thou hadst hearkened to my words, and stayed
With me, as I besought thee, when that strange
Desire of wand'ring this unhappy morn,
I know not whence possessed thee; we had then
Remained still happy, not as now, despoiled
Of all our good, shamed, naked, miserable.
Let none henceforth seek needless cause to approve
The faith they owe; when earnestly they seek
Such proof, conclude, they then begin to fail.

 To whom soon moved with touch of blame thus Eve.
What words have passed thy lips, Adam severe,
Imput'st thou that to my default, or will
Of wand'ring, as thou call'st it, which who knows
But might as ill have happened thou being by,
Or to thyself perhaps: hadst thou been there,
Or here th' attempt, thou couldst not have discerned
Fraud in the serpent, speaking as he spake;
No ground of enmity between us known,
Why he should mean me ill, or seek to harm.
Was I to have never parted from thy side?
As good have grown there still a lifeless rib.

Being as I am, why didst not thou the head
Command me absolutely not to go,
Going into such danger as thou saidst?
Too facile then thou didst not much gainsay,
Nay, didst permit, approve, and fair dismiss.
Hadst thou been firm and fixed in thy dissent,
Neither had I transgressed, nor thou with me.

    To whom then first incensed Adam replied.
Is this the love, is this the recompense
Of mine to thee, ingrateful Eve, expressed
Immutable when thou wert lost, not I,
Who might have lived and joyed immortal bliss,
Yet willingly chose rather death with thee:
And am I now upbraided, as the cause
Of thy transgressing? not enough severe,
It seems, in thy restraint: what could I more?
I warned thee, I admonished thee, foretold
The danger, and the lurking Enemy
That lay in wait; beyond this had been force,
And force upon free will hath here no place.
But confidence then bore thee on, secure
Either to meet no danger, or to find
Matter of glorious trial, and perhaps
I also erred in overmuch admiring
What seemed in thee so perfect, that I thought
No evil durst attempt thee, but I rue
That error now, which is become my crime,
And thou th' accuser. Thus it shall befall
Him who to worth in women overtrusting
Lets her will rule; restraint she will not brook,
And left to herself, if evil thence ensue,
She first his weak indulgence will accuse.

    Thus they in mutual accusation spent
The fruitless hours, but neither self-condemning,
And of their vain contést appeared no end.

CHRISTINA G. ROSSETTI

Christina Georgina Rossetti was born in London in 1830. Her masterpiece collection *Goblin Market and other poems* appeared in 1862 and won her instant acclaim. *The Prince's Progress and other poems* followed in 1866 and *Sing-Song: a nursery rhyme book* in 1872. Her many religious poems, 'Devotional Pieces', added to her huge popularity. She died in 1894.

CHRISTINA G. ROSSETTI

Upstairs, Downstairs . . .

'Downstairs I laugh, I sport and jest with all; / But in my solitary room above / I turn my face in silence to the wall; / My heart is breaking for a little love.' Upstairs, broken-hearted or not, 'in the fireless top back bedroom on the corner of the cracked washstand, on the backs of old letters Christina sat writing', according to Ford Madox Ford. Downstairs, a constant and copious stream of old friends from Naples and Rome, and new, English friends, among them Coventry Patmore, William Morris, John Ruskin, came to visit her expatriate father, Professor of Italian at King's College, London, and her adored Mamma, who presided with immense pride over her brilliant brood: Maria Francesca, who would write an acclaimed study of Dante; painter and poet Gabriel Charles Dante (who would, in a further tribute to the great poet, eventually call himself Dante Gabriel Rossetti); and William Michael, co-founder of the Pre-Raphaelite Brotherhood. It was in necessary isolation that Christina 'shut the door to face the naked truth' and carved out of the drama of her soul a poetry in which an intensity of feelings and emotions is captured with exquisite, painful precision. 'My heart dies inch by inch, the time grows old': the heart laid bare with a verbal scalpel. 'Nearly every one of her poems was an instance . . . of an emotion'. Her emotional power is not, however, for sentimentalists, as Philip Larkin makes clear. Rossetti's work, he writes, is 'unequalled for its objective expression of happiness denied and a certain unfamiliar steely stoicism'. The steely stoicism may have been due less to the bowing of her head in resignation than to the fact that the 'hope deferred' was deferred by the spiritually wilful Christina Georgina Rossetti (she very much liked her middle name), who turned away from love. Twice. Why? God, who requires a fine fidelity, would seem to have been responsible. 'I love, as you would have me, God the most; Would not lose Him, but you, must one be lost . . . / This say I, having counted up the cost': one of the sonnets from *Monna Innominata*, which, though written in the voice of Dante's Beatrice, clearly echoes Rossetti's own choice.

She settled early on her life's priority, one of deeply religious observance and passionate love of God. Men came second. Within that dialogue with self, in the battleground between soul and body, Rossetti, a girl of extreme temperament (she suffered a mental breakdown in early teenage years) and temper – her tantrums when young were formidable – found her poetic inspiration. God, and what Rossetti interpreted as His demands, inspired much of her poetry – both the love poetry and the devotional pieces, which number in the hundreds. Her first love, James Collinson, RA, whom she met when she was eighteen and who painted a darkly forbidding portrait of his young beloved (unlike Dante Gabriel's light-filled portrait of his sister as Mary at the Annunciation: *Ecce Ancilla Domini*) was rather unreliable spiritually. This was a fatal flaw in the eyes of the deeply religious Christina. Collinson changed his religion from that of committed Catholic to Protestant and then back again to Catholic. He was not perhaps a man for the long haul of the soul. Her second, perhaps deeper, affection was for Charles Bagot Cayley, from whom, aged thirty, she eventually received a proposal. Cayley was, alas, untroubled by any belief at all – which, of course, was the trouble. Virginia Woolf commented that if she were 'bringing a case against God', Christina Rossetti would be her first witness. Certainly there is something of Francis Thompson's 'The Hound of Heaven' in what Rossetti saw as God's unending pursuit: 'But all night long that voice spake urgently: / "Open to Me / . . . Rise, let Me in."' (From the poem 'Despised and Rejected'.)

Another poem, 'Dost Thou Not Care?', ends with Christ's reminder of His sacrifice, *'Did I not die for thee? / Do I not live for thee? leave Me tomorrow.'* A line which allows for no escape. Spiritual battles can be profoundly exhausting. In 'Weary in Well-Doing' resignation is a touch resentful: 'He broke my will from day to day, / He read my yearnings unexpressed / And said them nay . . . But, Christ my God, when will it be / That I may let alone my toil / And rest with Thee?'

Before she rested anywhere and despite her perpetual internal war Rossetti set about the publication of her work with a pragmatic professionalism, indeed worldliness, which may surprise many who link her with the nun of Amherst, Emily Dickinson. After the initial rejection of her poems Dickinson, the more fiercely intellectual of the two, declined with disdainful elegance to pursue publication, while neatly collating one poetic masterwork after another to be discovered after her death. Rossetti, on the other hand, aged only seventeen had two poems, 'Death's Chill Between' and 'Heart's Chill Between' (the titles clear indicators of what was to come), published in the prestigious literary weekly *Athenaeum*. She was declared the poet in the family, continued to write, upstairs, and was published in various magazines including the bizarrely named *The Germ*, a short-lived literary publication started by her brothers. Then in April 1862, when she was thirty-two, her debut collection *Goblin Market and other poems* was published by Macmillan and thus she entered literary history. The acclaim was immediate and deeply satisfying to its author, who, though she would follow it four years later with *The Prince's Progress and other poems*, which includes the beautiful hymn, 'A Christmas Carol' ('In the bleak mid-winter'), would never again in her many later collections stun her readers in quite the same way. Almost one hundred and fifty years after publication it stuns us still. It contains one of the most bewildering poems in literature, 'Goblin Market', which Edith Sitwell regarded as one of the most perfect poems written by a woman in the English language. Yet the poem which guaranteed its author immortality cannot be read, as she insisted to her less than convinced brother, William Michael, as simply a fairy tale. She was not a prude. Nor was she a nun. Her tragic sibling Dante Gabriel, with whom she shared a house, lived a not so secret life of debauchery. Recent biographies have pointed out that in the years 1859–60, and immediately prior to its publication, Christina Rossetti worked in a house for fallen women in Highgate – and worked so successfully that she was offered and declined the post of Principal. Though she was to live another thirty-two years and see 'Goblin Market' republished she never gave us any further guidance. Why should she? She knew what she'd done.

Christina Rossetti died from breast cancer in December 1894, aged sixty-four. Margaret Reynolds in *The Culture of Christina Rossetti* sounds a warning bell to all who claim definitive insight into this mysterious poet: 'Once upon a time Christina Rossetti was simple.' However, as we have discovered, that was 'Long ago and long ago', the last line of her aptly titled 'Maiden-Song'.

The Poems

Sisterhood, whether Pre-Raphaelite or not, is a challenging state, one which is quite different from that of brotherhood. It is never more challenging than in 'Goblin Market', the tale of two sisters, Lizzie and Laura. Laura, recklessly, 'with a golden curl', succumbs to the tones 'as smooth as honey' of the goblins' incessant cry to 'Come buy our orchard fruits, / Come buy, come buy:' and, having 'sucked and sucked and sucked the more . . . until her lips were sore', finds that yet her 'mouth waters still', and she wishes to 'Buy more'. Alas, the goblins seem to have disappeared and Lizzie, fearful that her sister will die from longing for the juice which has so entranced her, bravely sets out to find them. It is a dangerous endeavour, for when she does they 'Kicked and knocked her, / Mauled and mocked her'. Lizzie, 'white and golden' though dripping in their juice, never allows their poison to pass her lips. She rushes back to Laura and commands her to 'Eat me, drink me, love me; / Laura, make much of me: / For your sake I have braved the glen / and had to do with goblin merchant men'. Years later this tale of sisterly love ('there is no friend like a sister / In calm or stormy weather') is recounted by the repentant Laura, when both 'were wives / With children of their own'. It is a masterpiece of broken yet insistent rhythms so compelling as to seem as irresistible as the goblins' fruit, with their implied images of the Eucharist that mingle with nursery imagery and impossible-to-ignore luscious sexual innuendo. It is a Miltonian tale of temptation and triumph over evil – his *Comus* was widely believed to have been an inspiration. 'Goblin Market' itself is meant to have inspired *Alice's Adventures Underground*, whose author Charles Dodgson (Lewis Carroll) regarded Rossetti's tale as a work of genius. It is a telling compliment from the author of another surrealist masterpiece that also lends itself to a multitude of interpretations. The debate concerning Rossetti's poem has continued since publication. Is it, as the *Spectator* believed in 1862, a genuine childhood poem, as Arthur Rackham's enchanting 1933 illustrations would tend to confirm? Or, are the rather sinister later illustrations by George Gershinowitz and Martin Ware more truthful representations? Finally, and most controversially of all, do Kinuko Craft's 1973 illustrations for *Playboy* have a validity beyond George Bataille's concept of the phallic eye? The critic and poet Tom Paulin has ranked 'Goblin Market' alongside 'The Wreck of the *Deutschland*' as one of the greatest achievements of Victorian poetry. He is right.

Sisterhood is the subject of another disturbing poem from Rossetti, 'Sister Maude', who 'lurked to spy and peer' and who, through jealousy, brings about the death of her sister's lover and is then cursed in a brutal last line: 'But sister Maude, oh sister Maude, / Bide *you* with death and sin.'

The poem '"No, Thank You, John"' shows Rossetti in a rare, very rare, cool and witty mood. There was, evidently, an unfortunate John, a marine painter, who was despatched with some contempt: 'Here's friendship for you if you like; but love, – / No, thank you, John.'

I have, alas, for decades miscontrued one of her best-known and best-loved poems: 'When I am dead, my dearest, / Sing no sad songs for me . . . I shall not see the shadows, I shall not feel the rain; . . . Haply I may remember, / And haply may forget' does not denote 'happily' – it means by chance, which rather alters the mood!

The mood in 'Dost Thou Not Care?' is not open to misinterpretation of any kind. It is a despairing love song to Christ, an anguished cry: 'Dost Thou not love me, Lord, or care / For this mine ill?' 'Memory' is one of the poems which most merits Larkin's 'steely stoicism' insight. 'I faced the truth alone . . . None know the choice I made and broke my heart . . . I have braced my will / Once, chosen for once my part . . . I broke it at a blow . . . laid it cold . . .'. Will is perhaps the operative word in this remarkable poem of emotional self-destruction in the cause of the soul. The first stanza of 'Up-Hill' was, as Betty S. Flowers tells us, spoken in a sermon by the then lay-preacher in London, Vincent Van Gogh. Its last lines might have comforted that sad genius more: 'Will there be beds for me and all who seek? / Yea, beds for all who come.'

Goblin Market

Morning and evening
Maids heard the goblins cry:
'Come buy our orchard fruits,
Come buy, come buy:
Apples and quinces,
Lemons and oranges,
Plump unpecked cherries,
Melons and raspberries,
Bloom-down-cheeked peaches,
Swart-headed mulberries,
Wild free-born cranberries,
Crab-apples, dewberries,
Pine-apples, blackberries,
Apricots, strawberries; –
All ripe together
In summer weather, –
Morns that pass by,
Fair eves that fly;
Come buy, come buy:
Our grapes fresh from the vine,
Pomegranates full and fine,
Dates and sharp bullaces,
Rare pears and greengages,
Damsons and bilberries,
Taste them and try:
Currants and gooseberries,
Bright-fire-like barberries,
Figs to fill your mouth,

Citrons from the South,
Sweet to tongue and sound to eye;
Come buy, come buy.'

Evening by evening
Among the brookside rushes,
Laura bowed her head to hear,
Lizzie veiled her blushes:
Crouching close together
In the cooling weather,
With clasping arms and cautioning lips,
With tingling cheeks and finger tips.
'Lie close,' Laura said,
Pricking up her golden head:
'We must not look at goblin men,
We must not buy their fruits:
Who knows upon what soil they fed
Their hungry thirsty roots?'
'Come buy,' call the goblins
Hobbling down the glen.
'Oh,' cried Lizzie, 'Laura, Laura,
You should not peep at goblin men.'
Lizzie covered up her eyes,
Covered close lest they should look;
Laura reared her glossy head,
And whispered like the restless brook:
'Look, Lizzie, look, Lizzie,
Down the glen tramp little men.
One hauls a basket,
One bears a plate,
One lugs a golden dish
Of many pounds weight.
How fair the vine must grow
Whose grapes are so luscious;
How warm the wind must blow

Thro' those fruit bushes.'
'No,' said Lizzie: 'No, no, no;
Their offers should not charm us,
Their evil gifts would harm us.'
She thrust a dimpled finger
In each ear, shut eyes and ran:
Curious Laura chose to linger
Wondering at each merchant man.
One had a cat's face,
One whisked a tail,
One tramped at a rat's pace,
One crawled like a snail,
One like a wombat prowled obtuse and furry,
One like a ratel tumbled hurry skurry.
She heard a voice like voice of doves
Cooing all together:
They sounded kind and full of loves
In the pleasant weather.

Laura stretched her gleaming neck
Like a rush-imbedded swan,
Like a lily from the beck,
Like a moonlit poplar branch,
Like a vessel at the launch
When its last restraint is gone.

Backwards up the mossy glen
Turned and trooped the goblin men,
With their shrill repeated cry,
'Come buy, come buy.'
When they reached where Laura was
They stood stock still upon the moss,
Leering at each other,
Brother with queer brother;
Signalling each other,

Brother with sly brother.
One set his basket down,
One reared his plate;
One began to weave a crown
Of tendrils, leaves and rough nuts brown
(Men sell not such in any town);
One heaved the golden weight
Of dish and fruit to offer her:
'Come buy, come buy,' was still their cry.
Laura stared but did not stir,
Longed but had no money:
The whisk-tailed merchant bade her taste
In tones as smooth as honey,
The cat-faced purr'd,
The rat-paced spoke a word
Of welcome, and the snail-paced even was heard;
One parrot-voiced and jolly
Cried 'Pretty Goblin' still for 'Pretty polly;' –
One whistled like a bird.

But sweet-tooth Laura spoke in haste:
'Good folk, I have no coin;
To take were to purloin:
I have no copper in my purse,
I have no silver either,
And all my gold is on the furze
That shakes in windy weather
Above the rusty heather.'
'You have much gold upon your head,'
They answered all together:
'Buy from us with a golden curl.'
She clipped a precious golden lock,
She dropped a tear more rare than pearl,
Then sucked their fruit globes fair or red:
Sweeter than honey from the rock,

Stronger than man-rejoicing wine,
Clearer than water flowed that juice;
She never tasted such before,
How should it cloy with length of use?
She sucked and sucked and sucked the more
Fruits which that unknown orchard bore;
She sucked until her lips were sore;
Then flung the emptied rinds away
But gathered up one kernel-stone,
And knew not was it night or day
As she turned home alone.

Lizzie met her at the gate
Full of wise upbraidings:
'Dear, you should not stay so late,
Twilight is not good for maidens;
Should not loiter in the glen
In the haunts of goblin men.
Do you not remember Jeanie,
How she met them in the moonlight,
Took their gifts both choice and many,
Ate their fruits and wore their flowers
Plucked from bowers
Where summer ripens at all hours?
But ever in the noonlight
She pined and pined away;
Sought them by night and day,
Found them no more but dwindled and grew grey;
Then fell with the first snow,
While to this day no grass will grow
Where she lies low:
I planted daisies there a year ago
That never blow.
You should not loiter so.'
'Nay, hush,' said Laura:

'Nay, hush, my sister:
I ate and ate my fill,
Yet my mouth waters still;
Tomorrow night I will
Buy more:' and kissed her:
'Have done with sorrow;
I'll bring you plums tomorrow
Fresh on their mother twigs,
Cherries worth getting;
You cannot think what figs
My teeth have met in,
What melons icy-cold
Piled on a dish of gold
Too huge for me to hold,
What peaches with a velvet nap,
Pellucid grapes without one seed:
Odorous indeed must be the mead
Whereon they grow, and pure the wave they drink
With lilies at the brink,
And sugar-sweet their sap.'

Golden head by golden head,
Like two pigeons in one nest
Folded in each other's wings,
They lay down in their curtained bed:
Like two blossoms on one stem,
Like two flakes of new-fall'n snow,
Like two wands of ivory
Tipped with gold for awful kings.
Moon and stars gazed in at them,
Wind sang to them lullaby,
Lumbering owls forbore to fly,
Not a bat flapped to and fro
Round their rest:

Cheek to cheek and breast to breast
Locked together in one nest.

Early in the morning
When the first cock crowed his warning,
Neat like bees, as sweet and busy,
Laura rose with Lizzie:
Fetched in honey, milked the cows,
Aired and set to rights the house,
Kneaded cakes of whitest wheat,
Cakes for dainty mouths to eat,
Next churned butter, whipped up cream,
Fed their poultry, sat and sewed;
Talked as modest maidens should:
Lizzie with an open heart,
Laura in an absent dream,
One content, one sick in part;
One warbling for the mere bright day's delight,
One longing for the night.

At length slow evening came:
They went with pitchers to the reedy brook;
Lizzie most placid in her look,
Laura most like a leaping flame.
They drew the gurgling water from its deep;
Lizzie plucked purple and rich golden flags,
Then turning homewards said: 'The sunset flushes
Those furthest loftiest crags;
Come, Laura, not another maiden lags,
No wilful squirrel wags,
The beasts and birds are fast asleep.'
But Laura loitered still among the rushes
And said the bank was steep.

And said the hour was early still
The dew not fall'n, the wind not chill:
Listening ever, but not catching
The customary cry,
'Come buy, come buy,'
With its iterated jingle
Of sugar-baited words:
Not for all her watching
Once discerning even one goblin
Racing, whisking, tumbling, hobbling;
Let alone the herds
That used to tramp along the glen,
In groups or single,
Of brisk fruit-merchant men.
Till Lizzie urged, 'O Laura, come;
I hear the fruit-call but I dare not look:
You should not loiter longer at this brook:
Come with me home.
The stars rise, the moon bends her arc,
Each glowworm winks her spark,
Let us get home before the night grows dark:
For clouds may gather
Tho' this is summer weather,
Put out the lights and drench us thro';
Then if we lost our way what should we do?'

Laura turned cold as stone
To find her sister heard that cry alone,
That goblin cry,
'Come buy our fruits, come buy.'
Must she then buy no more such dainty fruit?
Must she no more such succous pasture find,
Gone deaf and blind?
Her tree of life drooped from the root:

She said not one word in her heart's sore ache;
But peering thro' the dimness, nought discerning,
Trudged home, her pitcher dripping all the way;
So crept to bed, and lay
Silent till Lizzie slept;
Then sat up in a passionate yearning,
And gnashed her teeth for baulked desire, and wept
As if her heart would break.

Day after day, night after night,
Laura kept watch in vain
In sullen silence of exceeding pain.
She never caught again the goblin cry:
'Come buy, come buy;' –
She never spied the goblin men
Hawking their fruits along the glen:
But when the noon waxed bright
Her hair grew thin and gray;
She dwindled, as the fair full moon doth turn
To swift decay and burn
Her fire away.

One day remembering her kernel-stone
She set it by a wall that faced the south;
Dewed it with tears, hoped for a root,
Watched for a waxing shoot,
But there came none;
It never saw the sun,
It never felt the trickling moisture run:
While with sunk eyes and faded mouth
She dreamed of melons, as a traveller sees
False waves in desert drouth
With shade of leaf-crowned trees
And burns the thirstier in the sandful breeze.

She no more swept the house
Tended the fowls or cows,
Fetched honey, kneaded cakes of wheat,
Brought water from the brook:
But sat down listless in the chimney-nook
And would not eat.

Tender Lizzie could not bear
To watch her sister's cankerous care
Yet not to share.
She night and morning
Caught the goblins' cry:
'Come buy our orchard fruits,
Come buy, come buy:' –
Beside the brook, along the glen,
She heard the tramp of goblin men,
The voice and stir
Poor Laura could not hear;
Longed to buy fruit to comfort her,
But feared to pay too dear.
She thought of Jeanie in her grave,
Who should have been a bride;
But who for joys brides hope to have
Fell sick and died
In her gay prime,
In earliest Winter time,
With the first glazing rime,
With the first snow-fall of crisp Winter time.

Till Laura dwindling
Seemed knocking at Death's door:
Then Lizzie weighed no more
Better and worse;
But put a silver penny in her purse,
Kissed Laura, crossed the heath with clumps of furze

At twilight, halted by the brook:
And for the first time in her life
Began to listen and look.

Laughed every goblin
When they spied her peeping:
Came towards her hobbling,
Flying, running, leaping,
Puffing and blowing,
Chuckling, clapping, crowing,
Clucking and gobbling,
Mopping and mowing,
Full of airs and graces,
Pulling wry faces,
Demure grimaces,
Cat-like and rat-like,
Ratel- and wombat-like,
Snail-paced in a hurry,
Parrot-voiced and whistler,
Helter skelter, hurry skurry,
Chattering like magpies,
Fluttering like pigeons,
Gliding like fishes, –
Hugged her and kissed her,
Squeezed and caressed her:
Stretched up their dishes,
Panniers, and plates:
'Look at our apples
Russet and dun,
Bob at our cherries,
Bite at our peaches,
Citrons and dates,
Grapes for the asking,
Pears red with basking
Out in the sun,

Plums on their twigs;
Pluck them and suck them,
Pomegranates, figs.' –

'Good folk,' said Lizzie,
Mindful of Jeanie:
'Give me much and many:' –
Held out her apron,
Tossed them her penny.
'Nay, take a seat with us,
Honour and eat with us,'
They answered grinning:
'Our feast is but beginning.
Night yet is early,
Warm and dew-pearly,
Wakeful and starry:
Such fruits as these
No man can carry;
Half their bloom would fly,
Half their dew would dry,
Half their flavour would pass by.
Sit down and feast with us,
Be welcome guest with us,
Cheer you and rest with us.' –
'Thank you,' said Lizzie: 'But one waits
At home alone for me:
So without further parleying,
If you will not sell me any
Of your fruits tho' much and many,
Give me back my silver penny
I tossed you for a fee.' –
They began to scratch their pates,
No longer wagging, purring,
But visibly demurring,
Grunting and snarling.

One called her proud,
Cross-grained, uncivil;
Their tones waxed loud,
Their looks were evil.
Lashing their tails
They trod and hustled her,
Elbowed and jostled her,
Clawed with their nails,
Barking, mewing, hissing, mocking,
Tore her gown and soiled her stocking,
Twitched her hair out by the roots,
Stamped upon her tender feet,
Held her hands and squeezed their fruits
Against her mouth to make her eat.
White and golden Lizzie stood,
Like a lily in a flood, –
Like a rock of blue-veined stone
Lashed by tides obstreperously, –
Like a beacon left alone
In a hoary roaring sea
Sending up a golden fire, –
Like a fruit-crowned orange tree
White with blossoms honey-sweet
Sore beset by wasp and bee, –
Like a royal virgin town
Topped with gilded dome and spire
Close beleaguered by a fleet
Mad to tug her standard down.

One may lead a horse to water,
Twenty cannot make him drink.
Tho' the goblins cuffed and caught her,
Coaxed and fought her,
Bullied and besought her,
Scratched her, pinched her black as ink,

Kicked and knocked her,
Mauled and mocked her,
Lizzie uttered not a word;
Would not open lip from lip
Lest they should cram a mouthful in:
But laughed in heart to feel the drip
Of juice that syrupped all her face,
And lodged in dimples of her chin,
And streaked her neck which quaked like curd.
At last the evil people
Worn out by her resistance
Flung back her penny, kicked their fruit
Along whichever road they took,
Not leaving root or stone or shoot;
Some writhed into the ground,
Some dived into the brook
With ring and ripple,
Some scudded on the gale without a sound,
Some vanished in the distance.
In a smart, ache, tingle,
Lizzie went her way;
Knew not was it night or day;
Sprang up the bank, tore thro' the furze,
Threaded copse and dingle,
And heard her penny jingle
Bouncing in her purse,
Its bounce was music to her ear.
She ran and ran
As if she feared some goblin man
Dogged her with gibe or curse
Or something worse:
But not one goblin skurried after,
Nor was she pricked by fear;
The kind heart made her windy-paced

That urged her home quite out of breath with haste
And inward laughter.

She cried 'Laura,' up the garden,
'Did you miss me?
Come and kiss me.
Never mind the bruises,
Hug me, kiss me, suck my juices
Squeezed from goblin fruits for you,
Goblin pulp and goblin dew.
Eat me, drink me, love me;
Laura, make much of me:
For your sake I have braved the glen
And had to do with goblin merchant men.'

Laura started from her chair,
Flung her arms up in the air,
Clutched her hair:
'Lizzie, Lizzie, have you tasted
For my sake the fruit forbidden?
Must your light like mine be hidden,
Your young life like mine be wasted,
Undone in mine undoing
And ruined in my ruin,
Thirsty, cankered, goblin-ridden?' –
She clung about her sister,
Kissed and kissed and kissed her:
Tears once again
Refreshed her shrunken eyes,
Dropping like rain
After long sultry drouth;
Shaking with aguish fear, and pain,
She kissed and kissed her with a hungry mouth.

Her lips began to scorch,
That juice was wormwood to her tongue,
She loathed the feast:
Writhing as one possessed she leaped and sung,
Rent all her robe, and wrung
Her hands in lamentable haste,
And beat her breast.
Her locks streamed like the torch
Borne by a racer at full speed,
Or like the mane of horses in their flight,
Or like an eagle when she stems the light
Straight toward the sun,
Or like a caged thing freed,
Or like a flying flag when armies run.

Swift fire spread thro' her veins, knocked at her heart,
Met the fire smouldering there
And overbore its lesser flame;
She gorged on bitterness without a name:
Ah! fool, to choose such part
Of soul-consuming care!
Sense failed in the mortal strife:
Like the watch-tower of a town
Which an earthquake shatters down,
Like a lightning-stricken mast,
Like a wind-uprooted tree
Spun about,
Like a foam-topped waterspout
Cast down headlong in the sea,
She fell at last;
Pleasure past and anguish past,
Is it death or is it life?

Life out of death.
That night long Lizzie watched by her,

Counted her pulse's flagging stir,
Felt for her breath,
Held water to her lips, and cooled her face
With tears and fanning leaves:
But when the first birds chirped about their eaves,
And early reapers plodded to the place
Of golden sheaves,
And dew-wet grass
Bowed in the morning winds so brisk to pass,
And new buds with new day
Opened of cup-like lilies on the stream,
Laura awoke as from a dream,
Laughed in the innocent old way,
Hugged Lizzie but not twice or thrice;
Her gleaming locks showed not one thread of grey,
Her breath was sweet as May
And light danced in her eyes.

Days, weeks, months, years
Afterwards, when both were wives
With children of their own;
Their mother-hearts beset with fears,
Their lives bound up in tender lives;
Laura would call the little ones
And tell them of her early prime,
Those pleasant days long gone
Of not-returning time:
Would talk about the haunted glen,
The wicked, quaint fruit-merchant men,
Their fruits like honey to the throat
But poison in the blood;
(Men sell not such in any town:)
Would tell them how her sister stood
In deadly peril to do her good,
And win the fiery antidote:

Then joining hands to little hands
Would bid them cling together,
'For there is no friend like a sister
In calm or stormy weather;
To cheer one on the tedious way,
To fetch one if one goes astray,
To lift one if one totters down,
To strengthen whilst one stands.'

Sister Maude

Who told my mother of my shame,
   Who told my father of my dear?
Oh who but Maude, my sister Maude,
   Who lurked to spy and peer.

Cold he lies, as cold as stone,
   With his clotted curls about his face:
The comeliest corpse in all the world
   And worthy of a queen's embrace.

You might have spared his soul, sister,
   Have spared my soul, your own soul too:
Though I had not been born at all,
   He'd never have looked at you.

My father may sleep in Paradise,
   My mother at Heaven-gate:
But sister Maude shall get no sleep
   Either early or late.

My father may wear a golden crown,
   My mother a crown may win;
If my dear and I knocked at Heaven-gate
   perhaps they'd let us in:
But sister Maude, oh sister Maude,
   Bide *you* with death and sin.

'No, Thank You, John'

I never said I loved you, John:
    Why will you teaze me day by day,
And wax a weariness to think upon
    With always 'do' and 'pray'?

You know I never loved you, John;
    No fault of mine made me your toast:
Why will you haunt me with a face as wan
    As shows an hour-old ghost?

I dare say Meg or Moll would take
    Pity upon you, if you'd ask:
And pray don't remain single for my sake
    Who can't perform that task.

I have no heart? – Perhaps I have not;
    But then you're mad to take offence
That I don't give you what I have not got:
    Use your own common sense.

Let bygones be bygones:
    Don't call me false, who owed not to be true:
I'd rather answer 'No' to fifty Johns
    Than answer 'Yes' to you.

Let's mar our pleasant days no more,
    Song-birds of passage, days of youth:
Catch at today, forget the days before:
    I'll wink at your untruth.

Let us strike hands as hearty friends;
    No more, no less; and friendship's good:
Only don't keep in view ulterior ends,
    And points not understood

In open treaty. Rise above
    Quibbles and shuffling off and on:
Here's friendship for you if you like; but love, –
    No, thank you, John.

Song

When I am dead, my dearest,
   Sing no sad songs for me;
Plant thou no roses at my head,
   Nor shady cypress tree:
Be the green grass above me
   With showers and dewdrops wet;
And if thou wilt, remember,
   And if thou wilt, forget.

I shall not see the shadows,
   I shall not feel the rain;
I shall not hear the nightingale
   Sing on, as if in pain:
And dreaming through the twilight
   That doth not rise nor set,
Haply I may remember,
   And haply may forget.

Dost Thou Not Care?

I love and love not: Lord, it breaks my heart
   To love and not to love.
Thou veiled within Thy glory, gone apart
   Into Thy shrine, which is above,
Dost Thou not love me, Lord, or care
   For this mine ill? –
I love thee here or there,
   I will accept thy broken heart, lie still.

Lord, it was well with me in time gone by
   That cometh not again,
When I was fresh and cheerful, who but I?
   I fresh, I cheerful: worn with pain
Now, out of sight and out of heart;
   O Lord, how long? –
I watch thee as thou art,
   I will accept thy fainting heart, be strong.

'Lie still,' 'be strong,' today; but, Lord, tomorrow,
   What of tomorrow, Lord?
Shall there be rest from toil, be truce from sorrow,
   Be living green upon the sward
Now but a barren grave to me,
   Be joy for sorrow? –
Did I not die for thee?
   Do I not live for thee? leave Me tomorrow.

Memory

I

I nursed it in my bosom while it lived,
   I hid it in my heart when it was dead;
In joy I sat alone, even so I grieved
    Alone and nothing said.

I shut the door to face the naked truth,
   I stood alone—I faced the truth alone,
Stripped bare of self-regard or forms or ruth
    Till first and last were shown.

I took the perfect balances and weighed;
   No shaking of my hand disturbed the poise;
Weighed, found it wanting: not a word I said,
    But silent made my choice.

None know the choice I made; I make it still.
   None know the choice I made and broke my heart,
Breaking mine idol: I have braced my will
    Once, chosen for once my part.

I broke it at a blow, I laid it cold,
   Crushed in my deep heart where it used to live.
My heart dies inch by inch; the time grows old,
    Grows old in which I grieve.

II

I have a room whereinto no one enters
   Save I myself alone:
   There sits a blessed memory on a throne
There my life centres;

While winter comes and goes—oh tedious comer!—
   And while its nip-wind blows;
   While bloom the bloodless lily and warm rose
Of lavish summer.

If any should force entrance he might see there
   One buried yet not dead,
   Before whose face I no more bow my head
Or bend my knee there;

But often in my worn life's autumn weather
   I watch there with clear eyes,
   And think how it will be in Paradise
When we're together.

A Christmas Carol

In the bleak mid-winter
   Frosty wind made moan,
Earth stood hard as iron,
   Water like a stone;
Snow had fallen, snow on snow,
   Snow on snow,
In the bleak mid-winter
   Long ago.

Our God, Heaven cannot hold Him
   Nor earth sustain;
Heaven and earth shall flee away
   When He comes to reign:
In the bleak mid-winter
   A stable-place sufficed
The Lord God Almighty
   Jesus Christ.

Enough for Him whom cherubim
   Worship night and day,
A breastful of milk
   And a mangerful of hay;
Enough for Him whom angels
   Fall down before,
The ox and ass and camel
   Which adore.

Angels and archangels
    May have gathered there,
Cherubim and seraphim
    Throng'd the air,
But only His mother
    In her maiden bliss
Worshipped the Beloved
    With a kiss.

What can I give Him,
    Poor as I am?
If I were a shepherd
    I would bring a lamb,
If I were a wise man
    I would do my part! –
Yet what I can I give Him,
    Give my heart.

Up-Hill

Does the road wind up-hill all the way?
    Yes, to the very end.
Will the day's journey take the whole long day?
    From morn to night, my friend.

But is there for the night a resting-place?
    A roof for when the slow dark hours begin.
May not the darkness hide it from my face?
    You cannot miss that inn.

Shall I meet other wayfarers at night?
    Those who have gone before.
Then must I knock, or call when just in sight?
    They will not keep you standing at that door.

Shall I find comfort, travel-sore and weak?
    Of labour you shall find the sum.
Will there be beds for me and all who seek?
    Yea, beds for all who come.

PERCY BYSSHE SHELLEY

Percy Bysshe Shelley was born into an aristocratic family in Sussex in 1792. Poet, playwright and courageous pamphleteer, his long poem *Queen Mab*, published in 1813 when he was twenty, was regarded as one of the most revolutionary poems in the language. *The Revolt of Islam* (1818), *The Mask of Anarchy* (1819), *Prometheus Unbound* (1820), his haunting odes and his final work *The Triumph of Life* (published posthumously in 1824) testify to his intellectual and lyric genius. He drowned in the Bay of Lerici in 1822.

PERCY BYSSHE SHELLEY

What Stopped Him?

Only death. 'I always go on until I am stopped,' he once wrote, 'and I am never stopped.' Youth! It was not wasted on young Percy Bysshe Shelley. He lived his short life in an ecstasy of being and creating – one and the same thing to Shelley. He was born on 4 August 1792 to Sir Timothy Shelley, MP for Horsham, Sussex, Whig aristocrat and a deeply religious man. He had high hopes for his brilliant and beautiful boy. Like many of his class he saw his son's future as a chronicle of a life foretold. Shelley, however, intended to write his own. Sir Timothy had bred an immortal – never a comfortable position for a father. His son believed poetry to be 'a fountain flowing with the waters of wisdom and delight', 'a sword of lightning, forever unsheathed'. He pursued the extreme not only in poetry and prose but also in his most emphatically unordinary life. If his father was abashed, so are we. The incandescence of his nature, his febrile sensitivity, the sometimes reckless intensity of his political and philosophical idealism, his fantastical dreams, his sublime intelligence – sharp as a blade – all astonish us and sometimes hint at the edge of madness. He began as he meant to go on.

In the nursery he was the thrilling brother of adoring sisters, whose chilblains he would eventually promise to cure by means of electrification. The family cat was perhaps a less willing victim. At Syon House, his preparatory school, where he was mercilessly bullied, he 'surprised' his school friends when, with gunpowder, he blew off the lid of his desk. At Eton, where he was again bullied, 'Mad' Shelley's rages were themselves electrifying (though he gained respect as a published novelist with the violent, passionate *Zastrozzi* – fee £40). At Oxford he horrified everyone by writing 'The Necessity of Atheism', its provocative conclusion: 'Every reflecting mind must allow that there is no proof of the existence of a Deity. QED.' He could perhaps have put it more subtly. He was sent down – atheism was dangerous, treacherous, blasphemous and therefore possibly criminal. Sir Timothy, horrified and himself fearful of legal proceedings, sent his communications to his son through legal channels. A furious Shelley disinherited himself by surrendering his claim on the family estate, Field Place, for an annuity of £2000, thus wounding himself and his father.

He found consolation with the Westbrook family, well-off coffee merchants. The daughters of the house, Eliza and Harriet, were enchanting and, after consideration of each, he ran away with Harriet, aged sixteen. They married and had two children, Ianthe and Eliza. Shelley seemed initially happy with Harriet: 'Love seems inclined to stay in the prison.' Alas, it would escape. For Shelley fell madly in love with another, the phrase, in this case, forensically accurate. Mary Godwin was the brilliant, beautiful daughter of philosopher William Godwin and Mary Wollstonecraft, author of *A Vindication of the Rights of Woman*, who had died shortly after her daughter's birth. Distraught by the possibility their love might be thwarted Shelley held out laudanum to the ashen-faced Mary. 'They wish to separate us, my beloved; but Death shall unite us.' Happily for us Mary resisted the laudanum and thus left us her strange masterpiece *Frankenstein*. She did not, however, resist Shelley. What sixteen-year-old could? She left home, as had Harriet. She didn't leave alone; fathers Beware! In case the couple might get lonely Shelley took her fifteen-year-old half-sister, Jane, with them. She, finding the name less than alluring, changed it to Claire – allurement being the *raison d'être* of Claire Clairmont. (She would practise it ruthlessly on Lord Byron, succeed briefly and be equally ruthlessly rejected. She would also become pregnant from her ten minutes of '*happy passion*' with Lord Byron.) William Godwin was, understandably, initially enraged. It is one thing to believe in free love, another matter altogether to have it practised on one's daughter. He soothed himself eventually. Aristocratic connections have a charm all their own. Free love came, as it always does, at a high price. Shelley was no lust-filled predator. He loathed grossness of any kind. However, his high romanticism about sexual love made him more dangerous and indeed more cruel than Byron – with whom you at least knew what you were getting. Consumed by his obsession with Mary, Shelley endeavoured to persuade Harriet, whom he did not wish to divorce (though their marriage was, as he cruelly explained to her, not one of passion), of the philosophical and moral rightness of his *true* passion for Mary. He failed, and in 1816 Harriet drowned herself. The heartbroken Westbrook family applied for custody of the children, as did Shelley. They both lost, and the children were fostered. The tragedy cast a long shadow. Few were well disposed to a declared atheist whose young wife and mother of his children had committed suicide, her heart broken by cruel infidelity. The reviews in 1818 of his long poem *The Revolt of Islam*, inspired by the French Revolution, were savage. Previously titled 'Laon and Cythna', it had been suppressed due to its perceived theme of incest. Though he declared in the preface, 'I have written fearlessly . . . I believe that Homer, Shakespeare, and Milton wrote with an utter disregard of anonymous censure', he was aware that his future in England, like his past, was bleak. In a sense he allowed himself to be hounded out of England, although not before writing one of the greatest lyrics in the language, 'Ozymandias', king of kings: 'Look on my works, ye Mighty, and despair!' The five years remaining to him were years of exile in Italy and of unbearable tragedy. His daughter with Mary, Clara, died in 1818 aged one; the following year his son William, aged three, died. He wrote on in virtual literary obscurity, with much of his work being published posthumously. In his last years he bequeathed us 'Julian and Maddalo', a precursor to Browning's dramatic monologues; the great metaphysical poem, 'The Cloud' ('I change, but I cannot die'); *The Mask of Anarchy* ('I met Murder on the way – / He had a mask like Castlereagh'); odes 'To the West Wind' ('tameless, and swift, and proud'), 'To a Skylark'

('Our sweetest songs are those that / tell of saddest thought'); 'Adonais', his passionate defence of Keats; and 'Epipsychidion'; the plays *The Cenci* and *Prometheus Unbound* (a sacred text to Yeats); and 'A Defence of Poetry', in which poets are declared to be 'the unacknowledged legislators of the world'.

He was in the midst of writing *The Triumph of Life* when his own ended. He drowned on 8 July 1822, aged twenty-nine, in a storm in the Bay of Lerici, having refused an offer of assistance from another boat. He'd designed his own, the *Don Juan* in honour of Byron. It had a built-in fault. When his body was recovered (a copy of Keats's 'Hyperion' in his pocket) he was cremated on the sands. His heart wouldn't burn. And that's the essence of Shelley. His heart was indestructible. *Cor Cordium*, heart of hearts, reads his gravestone. Probably literature's most truthful epitaph.

The Poems

'The poet and the man are two different natures.' Shelley, like Eliot, believed in that distance. Yet emotional self-expression is a prime characteristic of the Romantics, and Shelley was, as Harold Bloom notes, the greatest 'High Romantic' of them all. *Queen Mab*, printed but not published for fear of prosecution (the notes are as notorious as the poem), throws down the gauntlet: atheism, vegetarianism and free love are all praised. The lines we've taken tell us, sadly, that 'Even love is sold'. 'Ozymandias', his finest sonnet according to Richard Holmes, is the result of a challenge. Shelley and a friend had visited the British Museum's Egyptian exhibition and each agreed to write a sonnet. Only one is remembered; such is genius. 'Hymn to Intellectual Beauty' honours Byron, who enjoyed the recognition and success that eluded Shelley in his lifetime. 'I have lived too long near Lord Byron,' he said, 'and the sun has extinguished the glow worm.' Not quite, as time would prove.

'Julian [Shelley] and Maddalo [Byron]' is a conversation between the two poets – 'the child' is believed to be Allegra, Byron's daughter by Claire Clairmont. Love's terrible cost is told by 'the madman' who loved 'the lady who had left him', and though she returned had been destroyed by her. *The Mask of Anarchy* is not only a response to the Peterloo Massacre, in which a number of unarmed protestors were killed and over five hundred injured, it is also a Miltonian hymn to liberty and burns with a hatred of authority. 'Love's Philosophy', supposedly written to Sophia Stacey, a ward of Shelley's uncle who shared a house with them in Florence, is mischievous and sweet. It is also disconcerting, as Shelley was at the time in the midst of tragedy. More was to come. Shelley, Keats and Byron, a poetic constellation, were wiped out within a few years of each other. Keats, who did not much care for Shelley, was the first to die, aged twenty-five. 'Adonais', Shelley's tribute to him, is also a fierce attack on the critics who had caused Keats despair such that he would wish for an unmarked grave. 'Here lies one whose name was writ in water.' It was water that claimed Shelley who, strangely, as a schoolboy often quoted Southey's 'The Curse of Kehama': 'And water shall see thee / And fear thee, and fly thee / The waves shall not touch thee / As they pass by thee!' They did not flee him. He left unfinished, mid-sentence, 'Then, what is Life? / . . . Happy those for whom the fold' / Of', the poem which, according to Harold Bloom, persuades us is how Dante would sound, had he composed in English. The 550-line fragment, *The Triumph of Life*, is, according to Bloom, 'the most despairing poem, of true eminence, in the language . . . It would bewilder and depress us were it not for its augmented poetic power.' Shelley is buried beside Keats, in the Protestant Cemetery in Rome. 'Nothing of him that doth fade / But doth suffer a sea-change / Into something rich and strange'.

Queen Mab

[excerpt]

'All things are sold: the very light of Heaven
Is venal; earth's unsparing gifts of love,
The smallest and most despicable things
That lurk in the abysses of the deep,
All objects of our life, even life itself,
And the poor pittance which the laws allow
Of liberty, the fellowship of man,
Those duties which his heart of human love
Should urge him to perform instinctively,
Are bought and sold as in a public mart
Of undisguising selfishness, that sets
On each its price, the stamp-mark of her reign.
Even love is sold; the solace of all woe
Is turned to deadliest agony, old age
Shivers in selfish beauty's loathing arms,
And youth's corrupted impulses prepare
A life of horror from the blighting bane
Of commerce; whilst the pestilence that springs
From unenjoying sensualism, has filled
All human life with hydra-headed woes.'

Ozymandias

I met a traveller from an antique land
Who said: Two vast and trunkless legs of stone
Stand in the desert . . . Near them, on the sand,
Half sunk, a shattered visage lies, whose frown,
And wrinkled lip, and sneer of cold command,
Tell that its sculptor well those passions read
Which yet survive, stamped on these lifeless things,
The hand that mocked them, and the heart that fed:
And on the pedestal these words appear:
'My name is Ozymandias, king of kings:
Look on my works, ye Mighty, and despair!'
Nothing beside remains. Round the decay
Of that colossal wreck, boundless and bare
The lone and level sands stretch far away.

Hymn to Intellectual Beauty

[excerpt]

V

While yet a boy I sought for ghosts, and sped
  Through many a listening chamber, cave and ruin,
  And starlight wood, with fearful steps pursuing
Hopes of high talk with the departed dead.
I called on poisonous names with which our youth is fed;
    I was not heard—I saw them not—
    When musing deeply on the lot
Of life, at that sweet time when winds are wooing
    All vital things that wake to bring
    News of birds and blossoming,—
    Sudden, thy shadow fell on me;
I shrieked, and clasped my hands in ecstasy!

VI

I vowed that I would dedicate my powers
  To thee and thine—have I not kept the vow?
  With beating heart and streaming eyes, even now
I call the phantoms of a thousand hours
Each from his voiceless grave: they have in visioned bowers
    Of studious zeal or love's delight
    Outwatched with me the envious night—
They know that never joy illumed my brow
    Unlinked with hope that thou wouldst free
    This world from its dark slavery,
    That thou—O awful LOVELINESS,
Wouldst give whate'er these words cannot express.

VII

The day becomes more solemn and serene
    When noon is past—there is a harmony
    In autumn, and a lustre in its sky,
Which through the summer is not heard or seen,
As if it could not be, as if it had not been!
      Thus let thy power, which like the truth
      Of nature on my passive youth
Descended, to my onward life supply
    Its calm—to one who worships thee,
    And every form containing thee,
    Whom, SPIRIT fair, thy spells did bind
To fear himself, and love all human kind.

Julian and Maddalo: A Conversation

[excerpt]

'What Power delights to torture us? I know
That to myself I do not wholly owe
What now I suffer, though in part I may.
Alas! none strewed sweet flowers upon the way
Where wandering heedlessly, I met pale Pain
My shadow, which will leave me not again—
If I have erred, there was no joy in error,
But pain and insult and unrest and terror;
I have not as some do, bought penitence
With pleasure, and a dark yet sweet offence,
For then,—if love and tenderness and truth
Had overlived hope's momentary youth,
My creed should have redeemed me from repenting;
But loathèd scorn and outrage unrelenting
Met love excited by far other seeming
Until the end was gained . . . as one from dreaming
Of sweetest peace, I woke, and found my state
Such as it is.—'

The Mask of Anarchy

Written on the occasion of the massacre at Manchester

I
As I lay asleep in Italy
There came a voice from over the Sea
And with great power it forth led me
To walk in the visions of Poesy.

II
I met Murder on the way—
He had a mask like Castlereagh—
Very smooth he looked, yet grim;
Seven blood-hounds followed him:

III
All were fat; and well they might
Be in admirable plight,
For one by one, and two by two,
He tossed them human hearts to chew
Which from his wide cloak he drew.

IV
Next came Fraud, and he had on,
Like Eldon, an ermined gown;
His big tears, for he wept well,
Turned to mill-stones as they fell.

V
And the little children, who
Round his feet played to and fro,
Thinking every tear a gem,
Had their brains knocked out by them.

VI
Clothed with the Bible, as with light,
And the shadows of the night,
Like Sidmouth, next, Hypocrisy
On a crocodile rode by.

VII
And many more Destructions played
In this ghastly masquerade,
All disguised, even to the eyes,
Like Bishops, lawyers, peers, or spies.

VIII
Last came Anarchy: he rode
On a white horse, splashed with blood;
He was pale even to the lips,
Like Death in the Apocalypse.

IX
And he wore a kingly crown;
And in his grasp a sceptre shone;
On his brow this mark I saw—
'I AM GOD, AND KING, AND LAW!'

X
With a pace stately and fast,
Over English land he passed,
Trampling to a mire of blood
The adoring multitude,

XI

And a mighty troop around,
With their trampling shook the ground,
Waving each a bloody sword,
For the service of their Lord.

XII

And with glorious triumph, they
Rode through England proud and gay,
Drunk as with intoxication
Of the wine of desolation.

XIII

O'er fields and towns, from sea to sea,
Passed the Pageant swift and free,
Tearing up, and trampling down;
Till they came to London town.

XIV

And each dweller, panic-stricken,
Felt his heart with terror sicken
Hearing the tempestuous cry
Of the triumph of Anarchy.

XV

For with pomp to meet him came,
Clothed in arms like blood and flame,
The hired murderers, who did sing
'Thou art God, and Law, and King.

XVI

'We have waited, weak and lone
For thy coming, Mighty One!
Our purses are empty, our swords are cold,
Give us glory, and blood, and gold.'

XVII
Lawyers and priests, a motley crowd,
To the earth their pale brows bowed;
Like a bad prayer not over loud
Whispering—'Thou art Law and God.'—

XVIII
Then all cried with one accord,
'Thou art King, and God, and Lord;
Anarchy, to thee we bow,
Be thy name made holy now!'

XIX
And Anarchy, the Skeleton,
Bowed and grinned to every one,
As well as if his education
Had cost ten millions to the nation.

XX
For he knew the Palaces
Of our Kings were rightly his;
His the sceptre, crown, and globe,
And the gold-inwoven robe.

XXI
So he sent his slaves before
To seize upon the Bank and Tower,
And was proceeding with intent
To meet his pensioned Parliament

XXII
When one fled past, a maniac maid,
And her name was Hope, she said:
But she looked more like Despair,
And she cried out in the air:

XXIII

'My father Time is weak and gray
With waiting for a better day;
See how idiot-like he stands,
Fumbling with his palsied hands!

XXIV

'He has had child after child,
And the dust of death is piled
Over every one but me—
Misery, oh, Misery!'

XXV

Then she lay down in the street,
Right before the horses' feet,
Expecting, with a patient eye,
Murder, Fraud, and Anarchy.

XXVI

When between her and her foes
A mist, a light, an image rose,
Small at first, and weak and frail
Like the vapour of a vale:

XXVII

Till as clouds grow on the blast,
Like tower-crowned giants striding fast,
And glare with lightnings as they fly,
And speak in thunder to the sky,

XXVIII

It grew—a Shape arrayed in mail
Brighter than the viper's scale,
And upborne on wings whose grain
Was as the light of sunny rain.

XXIX
On its helm, seen far away,
A planet, like the Morning's, lay;
And those plumes its light rained through
Like a shower of crimson dew.

XXX
With step as soft as wind it passed,
O'er the heads of men—so fast
That they knew the presence there,
And looked,—but all was empty air.

XXXI
As flowers beneath May's footstep waken,
As stars from Night's loose hair are shaken,
As waves arise when loud winds call,
Thoughts sprung where'er that step did fall.

XXXII
And the prostrate multitude
Looked—and ankle-deep in blood,
Hope, that maiden most serene,
Was walking with a quiet mien:

XXXIII
And Anarchy, the ghastly birth,
Lay dead earth upon the earth;
The Horse of Death tameless as wind
Fled, and with his hoofs did grind
To dust the murderers thronged behind.

XXXIV

A rushing light of clouds and splendour,
A sense awakening and yet tender
Was heard and felt—and at its close
These words of joy and fear arose

XXXV

As if their own indignant Earth
Which gave the sons of England birth
Had felt their blood upon her brow,
And shuddering with a mother's throe

XXXVI

Had turnèd every drop of blood
By which her face had been bedewed
To an accent unwithstood,—
As if her heart had cried aloud:

XXXVII

'Men of England, heirs of Glory,
Heroes of unwritten story,
Nurslings of one mighty Mother,
Hopes of her, and one another;

XXXVIII

'Rise like Lions after slumber
In unvanquishable number,
Shake your chains to earth like dew
Which in sleep had fallen on you—
Ye are many—they are few.'

Love's Philosophy

I
The fountains mingle with the river
  And the rivers with the Ocean,
The winds of Heaven mix for ever
  With a sweet emotion;
Nothing in the world is single;
  All things by a law divine
In one spirit meet and mingle.
  Why not I with thine?—

II
See the mountains kiss high Heaven
  And the waves clasp one another;
No sister-flower would be forgiven
  If it disdained its brother;
And the sunlight clasps the earth
  And the moonbeams kiss the sea:
What is all this sweet work worth
  If thou kiss not me?

Adonais

[excerpt]

XXXVI

    Our Adonais has drunk poison—oh!
    What deaf and viperous murderer could crown
    Life's early cup with such a draught of woe?
    The nameless worm would now itself disown:
    It felt, yet could escape, the magic tone
    Whose prelude held all envy, hate, and wrong,
    But what was howling in one breast alone,
    Silent with expectation of the song,
Whose master's hand is cold, whose silver lyre unstrung.

XXXVII

    Live thou, whose infamy is not thy fame!
    Live! fear no heavier chastisement from me,
    Thou noteless blot on a remembered name!
    But be thyself, and know thyself to be!
    And ever at thy season be thou free
    To spill the venom when thy fangs o'erflow;
    Remorse and Self-contempt shall cling to thee;
    Hot Shame shall burn upon thy secret brow,
And like a beaten hound tremble thou shalt—as now.

XLII

    He is made one with Nature: there is heard
    His voice in all her music, from the moan
    Of thunder, to the song of night's sweet bird;
    He is a presence to be felt and known

In darkness and in light, from herb and stone,
Spreading itself where'er that Power may move
Which has withdrawn his being to its own;
Which wields the world with never-wearied love,
Sustains it from beneath, and kindles it above.

XLIII

He is a portion of the loveliness
Which once he made more lovely; he doth bear
His part, while the one Spirit's plastic stress
Sweeps through the dull dense world, compelling there,
All new successions to the forms they wear;
Torturing th' unwilling dross that checks its flight
To its own likeness, as each mass may bear;
And bursting in its beauty and its might
From trees and beasts and men into the Heaven's light.

XLIV

The splendours of the firmament of time
May be eclipsed, but are extinguished not;
Like stars to their appointed height they climb,
And death is a low mist which cannot blot
The brightness it may veil. When lofty thought
Lifts a young heart above its mortal lair,
And love and life contend in it, for what
Shall be its earthly doom, the dead live there
And move like winds of light on dark and stormy air.

XLV

The inheritors of unfulfilled renown
Rose from their thrones, built beyond mortal thought,
Far in the Unapparent. Chatterton
Rose pale,—his solemn agony had not
Yet faded from him; Sidney, as he fought
And as he fell and as he lived and loved

Sublimely mild, a Spirit without spot,
Arose; and Lucan, by his death approved:
Oblivion as they rose shrank like a thing reproved.

XLVI

And many more, whose names on Earth are dark,
But whose transmitted effluence cannot die
So long as fire outlives the parent spark,
Rose, robed in dazzling immortality.
'Thou art become as one of us,' they cry,
'It was for thee yon kingless sphere has long
Swung blind in unascended majesty,
Silent alone amid an Heaven of Song.
Assume thy wingèd throne, thou Vesper of our throng!'

XLVIII

Or go to Rome, which is the sepulchre,
Oh, not of him, but of our joy: 'tis nought
That ages, empires, and religions there
Lie buried in the ravage they have wrought;
For such as he can lend, – they borrow not
Glory from those who made the world their prey;
And he is gathered to the kings of thought
Who waged contention with their time's decay,
And of the past are all that cannot pass away.

The Triumph of Life

[excerpt]

. . .

The wild dance maddens in the van, and those
Who lead it—fleet as shadows on the green,

Outspeed the chariot, and without repose
Mix with each other in tempestuous measure
To savage music, wilder as it grows,

They, tortured by their agonizing pleasure,
Convulsed and on the rapid whirlwinds spun
Of that fierce Spirit, whose unholy leisure

Was soothed by mischief since the world begun,
Throw back their heads and loose their streaming hair;
And in their dance round her who dims the sun,

Maidens and youths fling their wild arms in air
As their feet twinkle; they recede, and now
Bending within each other's atmosphere,

Kindle invisibly—and as they glow,
Like moths by light attracted and repelled,
Oft to their bright destruction come and go,

Till like two clouds into one vale impelled,
That shake the mountains when their lightnings mingle
And die in rain—the fiery band which held

Their natures, snaps—while the shock still may tingle;
One falls and then another in the path
Senseless—nor is the desolation single,

Yet ere I can say *where*—the chariot hath
Passed over them—nor other trace I find
But as of foam after the ocean's wrath

Is spent upon the desert shore;—behind,
Old men and women foully disarrayed,
Shake their gray hairs in the insulting wind,

And follow in the dance, with limbs decayed,
Seeking to reach the light which leaves them still
Farther behind and deeper in the shade.

But not the less with impotence of will
They wheel, though ghastly shadows interpose
Round them and round each other, and fulfil

Their work, and in the dust from whence they rose
Sink, and corruption veils them as they lie,
And past in these performs what   in those.

Struck to the heart by this sad pageantry,
Half to myself I said—'And what is this?
Whose shape is that within the car? And why—'

I would have added—'is all here amiss?—'
But a voice answered—'Life!'—I turned, and knew
(O Heaven, have mercy on such wretchedness!) . . .

     . . .

ACTORS' NOTES

A selection of the poems in this book are read by the following actors on the attached CD.

Eileen Atkins graduated from the Guildhall School of Music and Drama and then starred at the Old Vic in *Richard II*, *The Tempest*, *Semi-Detached* with Laurence Olivier, and *Exit the King* with Alec Guinness. She has won the *Evening Standard* Best Actress award for *The Killing of Sister George*; the Variety Club Award for *Vivat! Vivat Regina!*; Olivier Best Actress awards for *The Unexpected Man* and *Honour*; a Special Citation from the New York Drama Critics' Circle for *A Room of One's Own*; the *Evening Standard* British Film Award for Best Screenplay for *Mrs Dalloway*; and the BAFTA Best Actress Award for the BBC's *Cranford*. She was awarded a CBE in 1990 and made a Dame Commander in 2001.

Nancy Carroll graduated from LAMDA and was cast as Ophelia at the Bristol Old Vic. She played major roles with the Royal National Theatre and the Royal Shakespeare Company in *The Winter's Tale*, *As You Like It*, *A Midsummer Night's Dream*, *Henry VI Parts 1 and 2*, *The False Servant*, *The Voysey Inheritance* and *The Man of Mode*; at the Almeida in *King Lear*; and in London's West End in *You Never Can Tell* and *The Enchantment*. Television credits include *Cambridge Spies* and *The Gathering Storm*; film credits include *Iris* and *An Ideal Husband*. In autumn 2008 she will star in the Almeida's production of *Waste* with David Morrissey.

Alan Cox played major roles with the Royal National Theatre and the Royal Shakespeare Company in *The Seagull*, *An Enemy of the People*, *The Winter's Tale*, and at the Almeida in *Earthly Paradise*. His film credits include *Young Sherlock Holmes* (as Dr Watson), *An Awfully Big Adventure*, *Mrs Dalloway*, *The Auteur Theory*, *Ladies in Lavender*; television credits include *Adam Bede*, *The Thin Blue Line* and *A Voyage Round My Father*. He is a much-respected theatre director, from 17th-century classics by Beaumont and Fletcher and Ben Jonson to the work of Pinter and Orton.

Charles Dance has played the major title roles with the Royal Shakespeare Company. He starred in the West End in *Long Day's Journey into Night* – opposite Jessica Lange – *Good* and *Shadowlands*, for which he won the London Critics' Circle Award for Best Actor. Television nominations and awards include a BAFTA nomination for *The Jewel in the Crown* and an Emmy nomination and Press Guild Award for Best Actor for *Bleak House*. Major films include *Plenty*, *White Mischief*, *Hilary and Jackie*, *Gosford Park* and *Kabloonak* – Best Actor Award at the Paris Film Festival. He wrote and directed the hugely successful *Ladies in Lavender*, for which Dame Judi Dench and Dame Maggie Smith were nominated for European Film Academy Awards.

Joanna David's major roles at the Royal National Theatre, the Royal Exchange, Manchester, and Chichester Festival Theatre include performances in *Copenhagen*, *The Importance of Being Earnest*, *Uncle Vanya* and *The Rivals*. In the West End she has starred in *The Cherry Orchard*; *Breaking the Code*; *A Voyage Round My Father* with Derek Jacobi, which transferred from the Donmar Warehouse; and, in 2008, in *A Ring Round the Moon*. Her television credits include *Sense and Sensibility*, *Rebecca*, *War and Peace*, *Pride and Prejudice*, *Inspector Morse*, *The Forsyte Saga*, *Rumpole of the Bailey* and *Bleak House*. She has just finished filming the series *Mutual Friends*.

Lindsay Duncan graduated from the Guildhall School of Music and Drama. Her major roles at the Royal Shakespeare Company, the Royal National Theatre and the Royal Court include award-winning performances in *Les Liaisons Dangereuses* opposite Alan Rickman – she won an Olivier Best Actress Award – and *Private Lives*, again opposite Alan Rickman – Olivier Best Actress Award and a Tony Award. In 2008 she starred in *That Face*, which transferred from the Royal Court to the West End. Television credits include the series *A Year in Provence*, *Traffik*, Alan Bleasedale's *GBH*, Stephen Poliakoff's *Shooting the Past* and the role of Lady Longford in the award-winning *Longford*. Also in 2008 she will play Margaret Thatcher for the BBC.

Edward Fox, a graduate of RADA, has won four BAFTA awards. His Most Promising Newcomer Award was followed by Best Supporting

Actor awards for *The Go-Between* in 1972, *A Bridge Too Far* in 1978 and *Edward and Mrs Simpson* in 1979, and in 1983 he was again nominated for *Gandhi*. His chilling lead performance in *The Day of the Jackal* brought worldwide fame. A consummate theatre actor, he starred in the legendary 1968 production of T. S. Eliot's *The Family Reunion* and garnered further acclaim in Simon Gray's *Quartermaine's Terms* in 1981, *The Old Masters* in 2005, Shaw's *You Never Can Tell* in 2006 and John Mortimer's two plays *Legal Fictions* in 2007–8. He was awarded an OBE in 2003 for his services to film and theatre.

Emilia Fox graduated from Oxford and immediately took the lead role as Mrs de Winter in the BBC's *Rebecca*. She then starred with Ralph Fiennes in the Almeida's acclaimed production of *Richard II* and played the title role in Chichester Festival Theatre's production of *Katherine Howard*. Her many television performances include roles in *King Henry VIII* with Ray Winstone, *Pride and Prejudice*, *Shooting the Past*, *Fallen Angel* and as Nikki Alexander in the hugely popular series *Silent Witness*. Her films include Roman Polanski's Oscar-winning *The Pianist*, *Ballet Shoes*, *Keeping Mum* and, in 2008, *Flashbacks of a Fool* with Mark Strong and Daniel Craig.

Robert Hardy joined the Royal Shakespeare Company after war service and Oxford. He played many seasons at Stratford and at the Old Vic, and starred in plays in the West End, on Broadway and in Paris. His television credits include *The Far Pavilions*; *Northanger Abbey*; *Middlemarch*; *All Creatures Great and Small*, for which he was nominated for a BAFTA; and *The Wilderness Years*, for which he won a Broadcasting Guild Award. His many films include *Frankenstein*, *Sense and Sensibility*, *Mrs Dalloway*, *An Ideal Husband* and four Harry Potter films. He is the author of *Longbow* and *The Great Warbow* and presented the television programmes *Longbow*, *Gordon of Khartoum* and *Horses in our Blood*. He was awarded a CBE in 1981.

Tom Hollander has appeared with Cheek by Jowl (*As You Like It*) and at the Royal National Theatre (*Landscape with Weapon*); the Donmar Warehouse (*Threepenny Opera*, *Hotel in Amsterdam*); the Royal Court (*Mojo*); on Broadway (*The Judas Kiss*); and at the Almeida (*Tartuffe*, *The Government*

Inspector, King Lear). Television includes *Absolutely Fabulous, Wives and Daughters, Cambridge Spies, The Lost Prince, John Adam and The Company* and, most recently, *Freezing*. His film appearances include *Bedrooms and Hallways, Martha, Meet Frank, Daniel and Laurence, Gosford Park, Enigma, The Lawless Heart, The Libertine, A Good Year, Pirates of the Caribbean* (II and III) and *Pride and Prejudice*. He recently completed *Valkyrie* (directed by Bryan Singer), *The Soloist* (dir. Joe Wright) and *In the Loop* (dir. Armando Ianucci).

Jeremy Irons graduated from the Bristol Old Vic and then starred in the West End in *Godspell* and at the Royal Shakespeare Company in the major roles, including *Richard II*. He made his Broadway debut in 1984 in Tom Stoppard's *The Real Thing* opposite Glenn Close, for which he won both the Drama League Award and a Tony Award for Best Actor. In 2006 he returned to the West End in *Embers* and in 2008 starred in *Never So Good* at the Royal National Theatre. His many film awards include an Academy Award and a Golden Globe for *Reversal of Fortune* and an Emmy and a Golden Globe for *Elizabeth I*.

Felicity Kendal starred at the Royal National Theatre in *Amadeus* and *Othello* opposite Paul Scofield, and *On the Razzle* and *Arcadia*. At the Old Vic and in the West End she has starred: opposite Alan Bates in *Much Ado About Nothing* and *Ivanov*, for which she won the *Evening Standard* Award for Best Actress; in *Jumpers*; *The Real Thing*; *Hapgood*; *Tartuffe*; *Heartbreak House*; *Indian Ink*; *Waste*; *The Seagull*; *Fallen Angels*; *Humble Boy*; Samuel Beckett's *Happy Days*; David Hare's *Amy's View* in 2007; and in *The Vortex* in 2008. Her many film and television performances include the seminal *Shakespeare Wallah* and the hugely popular series *The Good Life*. Her autobiography, *White Cargo*, was published in 1998. She was awarded a CBE in 1995.

Elizabeth McGovern made her film debut in Robert Redford's Oscar-winning *Ordinary People* and the following year she earned an Academy Award nomination for Best Supporting Actress for her performance in *Ragtime*. She won further acclaim in *The House of Mirth, The Wings of a Dove* and *The Truth*. Her work in classical theatre includes *A Midsummer Night's Dream, Three Sisters, Hamlet, As You Like It* and *The Misanthrope*. Her many television performances include *Tales from the Crypt, New Hampshire, The*

Scarlet Pimpernel and *The Changeling*. She has recently starred in *Daphne, A Room With A View* and the series *Freezing* with Tom Hollander and Hugh Bonneville.

Mark Strong graduated from the Bristol Old Vic and played major roles at the Royal National Theatre, the Royal Shakespeare Company and the Donmar Warehouse, where he performed in award-winning productions of *Uncle Vanya* and *Twelfth Night*, for which he was nominated for an Olivier. His television performances include *Low Winter Sun, Our Friends in the North, Anna Karenina, Emma* – in which he played Mr Knightly – and *The Long Firm*, for which he was nominated for a BAFTA and won a Broadcast Press Guild Award. His many film credits include *Fever Pitch*; *Sunshine*; *Stardust* with Robert De Niro; the Oscar-nominated *Syriana* with George Clooney; Roman Polanski's *Oliver Twist*; *Flashbacks of a Fool* with Daniel Craig; and Ridley Scott's *Body of Lies*.

Dominic West graduated from the Guildhall School of Music and Drama, and won the Ian Charleson Award for Best Newcomer for his performance in *The Seagull*. He played Edward Voysey in the Royal National Theatre's production of *The Voysey Inheritance*, starred in the West End production of *As You Like It* with Helen McCrory and Sienna Miller and in Tom Stoppard's award-winning *Rock 'n' Roll*. He plays McNulty in HBO's critically acclaimed and hugely successful TV show *The Wire*. Among his many starring roles in film: *28 Days, Mona Lisa Smile, The Forgotten* and *300*. Dominic is currently shooting *The Devil's Whore*, a four-part series for Channel 4 in which he plays Oliver Cromwell.

Greg Wise graduated from Glasgow's Royal Scottish Academy of Music and Drama. Among his major film performances are *The Judas Kiss, The Feast of July, The Disappeared, The Calling* and the role of John Willoughby in Ang Lee's Oscar-winning *Sense and Sensibility*. His television credits include *Elizabeth David: A Life in Recipes, The Moonstone*, the acclaimed production of *Madame Bovary* in which he played Rodolphe Boulanger and the award-winning BBC series *Cranford* with Dame Judi Dench and Dame Eileen Atkins. He has recently finished shooting *A Place of Execution* for ITV. He has been married to Emma Thompson since 2003 and they have a daughter.

COPYRIGHT ACKNOWLEDGEMENTS

COPYRIGHT ACKNOWLEDGEMENTS

SOURCE NOTES

Introduction, pp. 1–5

p. 1 'same as for love': Jay Parini, *Robert Frost: A Life* (William Heinemann, 1998)

p. 1 'that you have written it': Harold Bloom, *How to Read and Why* (Fourth Estate, 2001)

p. 1 'may differ from the author's and be equally valid – it may even be better': T. S. Eliot, *On Poetry and Poets* (Faber and Faber, 1957)

p. 1 'to startle us out of our sleep-of-death into a more capacious sense of life': Harold Bloom, *How to Read and Why*

p. 1 'trip . . . into the boundless': Jay Parini, *Robert Frost: A Life*

p. 1 'The Sound on the Page': Ben Yagoda, *The Sound on the Page* (Harper Resource, 2004)

p. 1 'somehow entangled in the words and fastened to the page': Robert Frost, quoted, Ben Yagoda ibid.

p. 1 'the something germinating in him for which he must find the words': T. S. Eliot, *On Poetry and Poets*

p. 1 'Footfalls echo in the memory/Down the passage which we did not take/Towards the door we never opened/Into the rose-garden': T. S. Eliot, *The Complete Poems and Plays of T. S. Eliot* (Faber and Faber, 1969)

p. 2 'My words echo/Thus, in your mind/But to what purpose/Disturbing the dust on a bowl of rose-leaves/I do not know': ibid.

p. 2 'begins in delight and ends in wisdom': Jay Parini, *Robert Frost: A Life*

p. 3 'gathered up the heart's desire of the world': R. F. Foster, *W. B. Yeats, A Life, I, The Apprentice Mage* (Oxford University Press, 1998)

p. 3 'thoughts, that breathe, and words, that burn': Thomas Gray, 'The Progress of Poesy'

p. 3 'the very image of life expressed in eternal truth': P. B. Shelley, 'A Defence of Poetry' in *The Major Works* (Oxford World's Classics, 2003)

p. 3 'When I am dead, my dearest,/ Sing no sad songs for me': Christina Rossetti, *The Complete Poems* (Penguin Classics, 2005)

p. 3 'old-fashioned tirade—/loving, rapid, merciless': Robert Lowell, 'Man and Wife', Frank Bidart, David Gewanter, DeSales Harrison (eds.), *Collected Poems* (Faber and Faber, 2003)

p. 4 'exactly as I talk': Edward E. Bostetter (ed.), *George Gordon, Lord Byron: Selected Works* (Holt, Rinehart & Winston Inc, 1951)

p. 4 'madmen who have made men mad': Lord Byron, *Childe Harold's Pilgrimage*, Canto III, v. XLIII, *The Collected Poems of Lord Byron* (Wordsworth Editions, 1994)

p. 4 'how Dante would have written had he written in English': Harold Bloom, *How to Read and Why*

p. 4 'poetry is the crown of imaginative literature . . . because it is a prophetic mode': ibid.

p. 4 'What though the field be lost?': John Milton, *Paradise Lost*, Book IX, line 26 (Oxford World's Classics, 2004)

p. 4 'its own place'; 'to reign in Hell, than serve in Heav'n': John Milton, *Paradise Lost*, Book I, lines 224, 263

p. 4 'a bridge thrown over time': P. B. Shelley, 'A Defence of Poetry' in *The Major Works*

p. 4 'ever accompanied by pleasure': ibid.

Elizabeth Bishop, pp. 9–14

p. 9 'Everything has written under it – I have seen it': Linda Anderson, Jo Shapcott (eds.), *Elizabeth Bishop: Poet of the Periphery* (Newcastle/ Longstalk Blood Axe Poetry Series 1, 2002)

p. 9 'the natural with the unnatural': ibid.

p. 9 'normal as sight . . . as artificial as a glass eye': ibid.

p. 9 'ice writing': ibid.

p. 9 'the always more successful surrealism of everyday life': ibid.

p. 9 'far away within the view': Bonnie Costello, *Elizabeth Bishop: Questions of Mastery* (Harvard University Press, 1991)

p. 9 'whose head has fallen over the edge of his bed,/whose face is turned so that the image of/the city grows down into his open eyes/ inverted and distorted': Elizabeth Bishop, *Complete Poems* (Chatto & Windus, 2004)

p.10 'I *think* (my italics) the man at the end is dead': Linda Anderson, Jo Shapcott (eds.), *Elizabeth Bishop: Poet of the Periphery*

p. 10 'heroic observations . . . his eyes fixed on facts and minute details, sinking or sliding giddily off into the unknown': Bonnie Costello, *Elizabeth Bishop: Questions of Mastery*

p. 10 'instinctive, modest, lifelong impersonation of an ordinary woman': Linda Anderson, Jo Shapcott (eds.), *Elizabeth Bishop: Poet of the Periphery*

p. 10 'Although I think I have a prize "unhappy childhood" almost good enough for text-books – please don't think I dote on it': ibid.

p. 10 'urge for order and dominance confronting a volatile inner life': Bonnie Costello, *Elizabeth Bishop: Questions of Mastery*

p. 11 'The art of losing isn't hard to master': Elizabeth Bishop, 'One Art', *Complete Poems*

p. 11 'Exile seems to work for me': Linda Anderson, Jo Shapcott (eds.), *Elizabeth Bishop: Poet of the Periphery*

p. 11 'Is it lack of imagination that makes us come/to imagined places, not just stay at home?/Or could Pascal have been not entirely right/about just sitting quietly in one's room? . . . Should we have stayed at home,/ wherever that may be?': Elizabeth Bishop, 'Questions of Travel', *Complete Poems*

p. 11 'I lost my mother's watch. And look! my last, or/next to last, of three loved houses went . . . I missed them, but it wasn't a disaster': Elizabeth Bishop, 'One Art', *Complete Poems*

pp. 11–12 'Suddenly, from inside,/came an *oh!* of pain/–Aunt Consuelo's voice . . . What took me/completely by surprise/was that it was *me:*/ my voice, in my mouth . . . I knew that nothing stranger/had ever happened, that nothing/stranger could ever happen': Elizabeth Bishop, 'In the Waiting Room', *Complete Poems*

p. 12 'genius is nothing more than childhood recovered at will': Charles Baudelaire, 'Le Peintre de la Vie Moderne' quoted in Bonnie Costello, *Elizabeth Bishop: Questions of Mastery*

p. 12 'beautifully formulated aesthetic-moral mathematics': Linda Anderson, Jo Shapcott (eds.), *Elizabeth Bishop: Poet of the Periphery*

The Poems

p. 13 'we are driving to the interior': Linda Anderson, Jo Shapcott (eds.), *Elizabeth Bishop: Poet of the Periphery*

p. 13 'loves that sense of constant re-adjustment': Elizabeth Bishop, 'The Gentleman of Shalott', *Complete Poems*

p. 13 'Eliot . . . used his "nerves" in "Prufrock"': C. K. Stead, *The New Poetic* (Continuum, 2005)

p. 13 'clear away what presses on the brain . . . alarms for the expected': Elizabeth Bishop, 'Love Lies Sleeping', *Complete Poems*

p. 13 'Le Roy, just how much are we owing?/Something I can't comprehend,/the more we got the more we spend': Elizabeth Bishop, 'Songs for a Colored Singer', *Complete Poems*

p. 13 'Life's like that . . .': Elizabeth Bishop, 'The Moose', *Complete Poems*

p. 13 'revise, revise, revise': Bonnie Costello, *Elizabeth Bishop: Questions of Mastery*

p. 13 'Just when I thought I couldn't stand it/another minute longer, Friday came': Elizabeth Bishop, 'Crusoe in England', *Complete Poems*

p. 13 'What one seems to want in art, in experiencing it, is the same thing necessary for its creation, a self-forgetting, perfectly useless concentration': Linda Anderson, Jo Shapcott (eds.), *Elizabeth Bishop: Poet of the Periphery*

p. 14 'Oh, but it is dirty!': Elizabeth Bishop, 'Filling Station', *Complete Poems*

p. 14 'Lose something every day . . . – Even losing you (the joking voice, a gesture/I love) I shan't have lied. It's evident/the art of losing's not too hard to master/though it may look like (*Write* it!) like disaster': Elizabeth Bishop, 'One Art', *Complete Poems*

Robert Browning, pp. 41–6

p. 41 'Within his work lies the mystery which belongs to the complex and within his life the much greater mystery which belongs to the simple': Ian Finlayson, *Browning: A Private Life* (HarperCollins, 2004)

p. 41 'There are two Brownings – an esoteric and an exoteric. The former never peeps out in society, and the latter has not a suggestion of *Men and Women*': Henry James quoted in G. K. Chesterton, *Robert Browning* (Macmillan, 1922)

p. 41 'on the dangerous edge of things./The honest thief, the tender murderer,/The superstitious atheist': Robert Browning, 'Bishop Blougram's Apology', *Selected Poems* (Penguin Classics, 2004)

p. 41 'from a sense of guilt . . . the utilisation of a deed in order to rationalise this feeling': Sigmund Freud, *Writings on Art and Literature* (Penguin, 1985)

p. 41 'You understand me: I'm a beast, I know': Robert Browning, 'Fra Lippo Lippi', *Selected Poems*

p. 41 '"Little else," he said, "was worth study"': J. W. Harper (ed.), *Browning: 'Men and Women' and Other Poems* (J. M. Dent & Sons Ltd, 1975)

p. 41 'considered from a point of view of creator of character [Browning] ranks next to him who made Hamlet': Douglas Dunn (ed.), *Robert Browning, Poems* (Faber and Faber, 2004)

p. 42 'while it gave him knowledge of everything else left him in ignorance of the ignorance of the world': Ian Finlayson, *Browning: A Private Life*

p. 42 'the passionate impatient struggles of a boy towards truth and love . . . growing pains accompanied by temporary distortion of the soul also': Maisie Ward, *Robert Browning and His World: The Private Face* (Cassell & Company Ltd, 1967)

p. 42 'the singular courage to decline to be rich': Ian Finlayson, *Browning: A Private Life*

p. 42 'My whole scheme of life . . . with its wants – material wants at least – was closely cut down and long ago calculated . . . So for my own future way in the world I have always refused to care': Ian Finlayson, *Browning: A Private Life*

p. 42 'laughed my Paracelsus to scorn': ibid.

p. 43 'I love your verses with all my heart': Douglas Dunn (ed.), *Robert Browning, Poems*

p. 43 'Determined, dared, and done': Christopher Smart, 'A Song to David'

p. 43 '"Do you object to all this adulation?" he was asked once when surrounded by admirers. "Object to it? I've waited forty years for it!"': Maisie Ward, *Robert Browning and His World: The Private Face*

p. 44 'A good many oddities and a good many great writers have been entombed in the Abbey but none of the odd ones have been so great and none of the great ones have been so odd': Ian Finlayson, *Browning: A Private Life*

The Poems

p. 45 'poet of desire': Ian Finlayson, *Browning: A Private Life*

p. 45 'John Bayley agrees': John Bayley, *The Power of Delight: A Lifetime in Literature* (W. W. Norton & Company, 2005)

p. 45 'enchanted . . . by the astonishing concentration of desire': ibid.

p. 45 'the Corruption of Man's Heart': Robert Browning, 'Gold Hair: A Story of Pornic', *Selected Poems*

p. 45 'listens in to his universe': Cecil Day Lewis, *A Hope for Poetry* (Blackwell, 1942)

p. 45 'Just for a handful of silver he left us,/Just for a riband to stick in his coat': Robert Browning, 'The Lost Leader', *Selected Poems*

p. 45–6 'It was roses, roses, all the way': Robert Browning, 'The Patriot', *Selected Poems*

p. 46 'Grow old along with me!/The best is yet to be': Robert Browning, 'Rabbi Ben Ezra', *The Poems of Robert Browning* (Wordsworth Editions, 1994)

p. 46 'For sudden the worst turns the best to the brave . . . Then a light, then thy breast,/O thou soul of my soul! I shall clasp thee again,/And with God be the rest!': Robert Browning, 'Prospice', *The Poems of Robert Browning*

Lord Byron, pp. 71–6

p. 71 'I will cut a swathe through the world or perish in the attempt': Fiona MacCarthy, *Byron: Life and Legend* (Faber and Faber, 2002)

p. 71 'Two men have died within our recollection, who had raised themselves, each in his own department, to the height of glory. One of them died at Longwood, the other at Missolonghi': Thomas Babington Macaulay, *Essays*, vol. 1 (Longmans, Green and Co., 1866)

p. 71 'the noblest spirit in Europe': Carlyle quoted in Bertrand Russell, *A History of Western Philosophy* (George Allen & Unwin, 1949)

p. 71 'the poetry projected a Personality – a personality Napoleonic in its insatiability and capacity for ruinous defeat': John Updike, *Due Considerations* (Hamish Hamilton, 2007)

p. 72 'he was a catalogue of false positions. His brain was male, his character was feminine': Harold Nicolson quoted in Fiona MacCarthy, *Byron: Life and Legend*

p. 72 'I hate a fellow who's all author': John Bayley, *The Power of Delight: A Lifetime in Literature* (W. W. Norton & Company, 2005)

p. 72 'I can never recast anything . . . I am like the Tiger, if I miss at first spring/I go back growling to my Jungle again – But if I *do* hit – it is crushing!': Lord Byron, *The Collected Poems of Lord Byron* (Wordsworth Editions, 1994)

p. 73 'woke up and found himself famous': Fiona MacCarthy, *Byron: Life and Legend*

p. 73 'It is only the self that he invented that he understood perfectly': T. S. Eliot, *On Poetry and Poets* (Faber and Faber, 1957)

p. 73 'was the unique object of his own attention': Stendhal quoted in André Maurois, *Byron* (Jonathan Cape, 1930)

p. 73 'mad – bad – and dangerous to know': Lady Caroline Lamb quoted in Fiona MacCarthy, *Byron: Life and Legend*

p. 73 'the great object in life is Sensation'; 'craving void': Edward E. Bostetter (ed.), *George Gordon, Lord Byron: Selected Works* (Holt, Rinehart & Winston Inc., 1951)

p. 73 'The Last Attachment': Iris Origo, *The Last Attachment* (Jonathan Cape/John Murray, 1949)

p. 74 'for which he could find no parallel in English literature': T. S. Eliot, *On Poetry and Poets*

p. 74 'is now one polished horde,/Formed of two mighty tribes, the Bores and the Bored': Lord Byron, *Don Juan*, Canto XVI, v. XCVI, *The Collected Poems of Lord Byron*

p. 74 'If I laugh at any mortal thing/'Tis that I may not weep': Lord Byron, *Don Juan*, Canto IV, v. IV, *The Collected Poems of Lord Byron*

The Poems

p. 75 'Mr Dallas has place in your hands a manuscript poem which he tells me you do not object to publishing': Lord Byron quoted in Fiona MacCarthy, *Byron: Life and Legend*

p. 75 'The wandering outlaw of his own dark mind': Lord Byron, *Childe Harold's Pilgrimage*, Canto III, v. III, *The Collected Poems of Lord Byron*

p. 75 'Conqueror and captive of the earth': Lord Byron, *Childe Harold's Pilgrimage*, Canto III, v. XXXVII, *The Collected Poems of Lord Byron*

p. 75 'the madmen who have made men mad': Lord Byron, *Childe Harold's Pilgrimage*, Canto III, v. XLIII, *The Collected Poems of Lord Byron*

p. 75 'Then fare thee well, Fanny/Now doubly undone/To prove false unto many/As faithless to one/Thou art past all re-calling . . .'; Lord Byron, 'When we two parted', Edward E. Bostetter (ed.) *George Gordon, Lord Byron: Selected Works*

p. 76 'I'd like to know who's been ravished . . . I've been more ravished myself than anybody since the Trojan War!': Edward E. Bostetter (ed.), *George Gordon, Lord Byron: Selected Works*

p. 76 'Man's love is of his life a thing apart,/'Tis woman's whole existence': Lord Byron, *Don Juan*, Canto I, v. CXCIV

p. 76 'The emotion is hatred. Hatred of hypocrisy': T. S. Eliot, *On Poetry and Poets*

p. 76 'without straining hard to versify rattle on exactly as I talk/With anybody in a ride or walk': Edward E. Bostetter (ed.), introduction to *George Gordon, Lord Byron: Selected Works*

p. 76 'each other, not divorced, but dead': Lord Byron, *Don Juan*, Canto I, v. XXVI

p. 76 'At *fifty* love for love is rare': Lord Byron, *Don Juan*, Canto I, v. CVIII

p. 76 'It may be profligate . . . but is it not life? Is it not the thing?': Edward E. Bostetter (ed.), *George Gordon, Lord Byron: Selected Works*

p. 76 'Sorrow is knowledge': Lord Byron, *Manfred, Collected Poems of Lord Byron*

Robert Frost, pp. 103–107

p. 103 'I have to say that my Frost […] In sum, he is a terrifying poet': Lionel Trilling quoted in Jay Parini, *Robert Frost: A Life* (Heinemann, 1998)

p. 103 'I'd rather be taken for brave than anything else': Lawrence Thompson (ed.), *Selected Letters of Robert Frost* (Jonathan Cape, 1965)

p. 103 'begins in delight and ends in wisdom': Robert Frost, 'The Figure a Poem Makes', *The Collected Poems of Robert Frost* (Amereon House/Buckaneer Books Inc., 1986)

p. 103 'acquainted with the night': Edward Connery Lathem (ed.), *The Poetry of Robert Frost* (Vintage, 2001)

p. 104 'Inflexible ambition trains us best': Jay Parini, *Robert Frost: A Life*

p. 104 'more Greek and Latin than either Eliot or Pound': John Updike, *Due Considerations* (Hamish Hamilton, 2007)

p. 104 'trip the reader head foremost into the boundless . . . Forward, you understand, and in the dark': Jay Parini, *Robert Frost: A Life*

p. 104 'Frost's is a signal from a far distant station . . . the fuel – grief and reason': Joseph Brodsky, *On Grief and Reason, Essays* (Farrar, Straus, and Giroux, 1995)

p. 104 'cutting along a nerve': Jay Parini, *Robert Frost: A Life*

p. 104 'there is a secret genius between the lines': ibid.

p. 105 'I teach myself my own take on the world'; 'I sit there radiating poetry': ibid.

p. 105 'Love is all. Romantic love – as in stories and poems. I tremble with it': ibid.

p. 105 'I can't touch my mind with a memory of any kind. I can't touch my skin': ibid.

p. 105 'God damn me when he gets around to it': ibid.

p. 105 'I would have written of me on my stone: I had a lover's quarrel with the world': ibid.

The Poems

p. 106 'If [when] you read my poem – you heard a voice, that would be to my liking . . . the gold in the ore is the sound': Robert Frost, 'The Figure a Poem Makes', *The Collected Poems of Robert Frost*

p. 106 'I don't know': 'A Servant to Servants', Edward Connery Lathem (ed.), *The Poetry of Robert Frost*

p. 106 'Neither refused the meeting': '"Out, Out—"', Edward Connery Lathem (ed.), *The Poetry of Robert Frost*

p. 106 'And they, since they/Were not the one dead, turned to their affairs': ibid.

p. 106 'Before I built a wall I'd ask to know/What I was walling in or walling out': 'Mending Wall', Edward Connery Lathem (ed.), *The Poetry of Robert Frost*

p. 106 'an appetite for independence [which] was fierce and expressed itself in a reiterated belief in his rights to limits: his defences, his fences, his freedom were all interdependent': Heaney quoted in Jay Parini, *Robert Frost: A Life*

p. 106 'momentary stay against confusion': Jay Parini, *Robert Frost: A Life*

p. 107 'And to do that to birds was why she came': 'Never Again Would Birds' Song be the Same', Edward Connery Lathem (ed.), *The Poetry of Robert Frost*

p. 107 'miles to go': 'Stopping by Woods on a Snowy Evening', Edward Connery Lathem (ed.), *The Poetry of Robert Frost*

Robert Lowell, pp. 127–32

p. 127 'Seeing less than others can be a great strain': Ian Hamilton, *Robert Lowell, A Biography* (Faber and Faber, 1982)

p. 127 'Looking back over thirty years of published work my impression is that the thread that strings the work together is autobiography': Orhan Pamuk, *Paris Review*, vol. 2 (Canongate, 2007)

p. 127 'The Lowell family itself was a more potent inspiration than any literature': John Bayley, *The Power of Delight: A Lifetime in Literature* (W. W. Norton & Company, 2005)

p. 127 'how far one can go too far': Angela Partington (ed.), *Oxford Dictionary of Quotations* (Oxford University Press, 1992)

p. 127 'you want the reader to say, this is true'; 'to believe he was getting the *real* Robert Lowell': Orhan Pamuk, *Paris Review*, vol.2

p. 127 'who hadn't a mean bone, an original bone or a funny bone in his body': Ian Hamilton, *Robert Lowell, A Biography*

p. 127 'Becoming ourselves,/we lose our nerve for children': 'To Mother', Frank Bidart, David Gewanter (eds.), *Robert Lowell: Collected Poems* (Farrar, Straus and Giroux, 2007)

p. 128 'she saw her husband as a valet sees through a master': 'Unwanted', Frank Bidart, David Gewanter (eds.), *Robert Lowell: Collected Poems*

p. 128 'until in his forties his soul went underground': '91 Revere Street', Frank Bidart, David Gewanter (eds.), *Robert Lowell: Collected Poems*

p. 128 'always inside me is the child who died': Ian Hamilton, *Robert Lowell, A Biography*

p. 128 'If your son is as you have described him,/he is an incurable schizophrenic': 'Unwanted', Frank Bidart, David Gewanter (eds.), *Robert Lowell: Collected Poems*

p. 128 'I believed I could stop cars and paralyze their forces by merely standing in the middle of the highway; . . . that I was the reincarnation of The Holy Ghost – To have known the glory, violence and banality of such an experience is corrupting': Ian Hamilton, *Robert Lowell, A Biography*

p. 128 'we really haven't any room – you'd have to pitch a tent on the lawn': Orhan Pamuk, *Paris Review*, vol. 2

p. 128 'It's such a miracle if you get lines that are halfway right': ibid.

p. 129 'You didn't write, you *re*-wrote': Randall Jarrell quoted in Frank Bidart, David Gewanter (eds.), *Robert Lowell: Collected Poems*

p. 129 'The Lord survives the rainbow of His will': 'The Quaker Graveyard in Nantucket', Frank Bidart, David Gewanter (eds.), *Robert Lowell: Collected Poems*

p. 129 'Dear Mr President, I very much regret that I must refuse the opportunity you have afforded me in your communication of August the 6th 1943 for service in the armed forces': Ian Hamilton, *Robert Lowell, A Biography*

p. 129 'I'm in for refusing to kill': ibid.

p. 129–30 'I'd been on tour and reading aloud and more and more I was simplifying my poems': Orhan Pamuk, *Paris Review*, vol. 2

p. 130 'confessional poetry': ibid.

p. 130 '(But our beginnings never know our ends!)': T. S. Eliot, 'Portrait of a Lady', *Collected Poems* (Faber and Faber, 1936)

The Poems

p. 131 'It's better to get your emotions out in a Macbeth than in a confession': Orhan Pamuk, *Paris Review*, vol. 2

p. 131 'They relinquish everything to serve the Republic': translation of the Latin epigraph to 'For the Union Dead', Frank Bidart, David Gewanter (eds.), *Robert Lowell: Collected Poems*

p. 131 'the unwilling haunted saintliness of a man who was repaying the moral debts of tens of generations of ancestors': Norman Mailer, *The Armies of the Night* (Plume, 1994)

p. 131 'once/nineteen, the youngest ensign in his class,/he was "the old man" of a gunboat on the Yangtze': 'Commander Lowell', Frank Bidart, David Gewanter (eds.), *Robert Lowell: Collected Poems*

p. 131 'tranquillized *Fifties*,/and I am forty . . .': 'Memories of West Street and Lepke', Frank Bidart, David Gewanter (eds.), *Robert Lowell: Collected Poems*

p. 131 'manic statement,/telling off the state and president': ibid.

p. 131 'the electric chair—/hanging like an oasis in his air/of lost connections . . .': ibid.

p. 132 'are the stamp': John Donne quoted in *Larkin at Sixty* (Faber and Faber, 1982)

p. 132 'My mind's not right': 'Skunk Hour', Frank Bidart, David Gewanter (eds.), *Robert Lowell: Collected Poems*

p. 132 'a locked razor': 'Waking In The Blue', Frank Bidart, David Gewanter (eds.), *Robert Lowell: Collected Poems*

p. 132 'old-fashioned tirade—/loving, rapid, merciless—/breaks like the Atlantic Ocean on my head': 'Man and Wife', Frank Bidart, David Gewanter (eds.), *Robert Lowell: Collected Poems*

p. 132 'the monstrous meanness of his lust': 'To Speak of Woe That Is in Marriage', Frank Bidart, David Gewanter (eds.), *Robert Lowell: Collected Poems*

p. 132 'I enjoyed writing about my life more than living it': Ian Hamilton, *Robert Lowell, A Biography*

p. 132 'Alas, I can only tell my own story': Frank Bidart, David Gewanter (eds.), *Robert Lowell: Collected Poems*

p. 132 'Yet why not say what happened?/Pray for the grace of accuracy . . . We are poor passing facts,/warned by that to give/each figure in the photograph/his living name': 'Epilogue', Frank Bidart, David Gewanter (eds.), *Robert Lowell: Collected Poems*

John Milton, pp. 151–57

p. 151 'Allow me to use big language with you. You ask what I am thinking of? I am thinking of immortality. What am I doing? Growing my wings and meditating flight. But as yet our Pegasus raises himself on very tender wings. Let us be lowly wise.': James Vinson (ed.), *Great Writers of the English Language: Poets* (Macmillan, 1979)

p. 151 'long choosing, and beginning late': John Milton, *Paradise Lost*, Book IX, line 26 (Oxford World's Classics, 2004)

p. 151 'to leave something so written to after times as they should not willingly let it die': Douglas Bush (ed.), John Milton, *Complete Poetical Works* (Oxford University Press, 1990)

p. 151 'Milton is the deity of prescience': Justin Wintle, Richard Kenin (eds.), *Penguin Concise Dictionary of Biographical Quotation* (Penguin, 1978)

p. 151 'a direct line which can be traced from Virgil': Ted Hughes, speech, Arvon Foundation event

p. 152 'honest haughtiness': Douglas Bush (ed.), John Milton, *Complete Poetical Works*

p. 152 'corporal correction': Arthur Waugh (ed.), Samuel Johnson, *Lives of the Poets*, vol. 1, (Kegan Paul, Trench, Trubner & Co., 1896)

p. 152 'come, and trip it as ye go/on the light fantastic toe': Douglas Bush (ed.), John Milton, *Complete Poetical Works*

p. 152 'be not cosen'd with that same vaunted name Virginity . . . if you let slip time, like a neglected rose/it withers on the stalk with languished head ... Beauty is nature's brag': Douglas Bush (ed.), John Milton, *Complete Poetical Works*

p. 152 'a clergyman must subscribe slave ... bought and begun with servitude and forswearing': Arthur Waugh (ed.), Samuel Johnson, *Lives of the Poets*, vol. 1

p. 152 'Thoughts of Obedience, whether Canonical or Civil, raised his indignation': ibid.

p. 153 'deadly hatred which he bore to bigots and tyrants'; 'the faith which he so sternly kept with his country': Thomas Babington Macaulay, *Essays*, vol. 1 (Longman, Green and Co., London, 1866)

p. 153 'the Bill of Rights owes more to John Milton than to John Locke': Professor Myron Taylor in James Vinson (ed.), *Great Writers of the English Language: Poets*

p. 153 'the poet honoured her memory with a poor sonnet': Arthur Waugh (ed.), Samuel Johnson, *Lives of the Poets*, vol. 1

p. 153 'But O as to embrace me she enclined,/I wak'd, she fled, and day brought back my night': Douglas Bush (ed.), John Milton, *Complete Poetical Works*

p. 153–4 'The most important fact about Milton for my purpose is his blindness ... it would seem indeed to have helped him concentrate on what he could do best': T. S. Eliot, *On Poetry and Poets* (Faber and Faber, 1957)

p. 154 'stand and wait': 'Milton, On His Blindness', Douglas Bush (ed.), John Milton, *Complete Poetical Works*

p. 154 'unsinkable, there may be no larger triumph of the visionary will in western literature': Harold Bloom, *The Western Canon* (Riverhead, 1994)

p. 154 'calm of mind, all passion spent': *Samson Agonistes*, Douglas Bush (ed.), John Milton, *Complete Poetical Works*

Paradise Lost

p. 155 'No man ever wished *Paradise Lost* were longer': Arthur Waugh (ed.), Samuel Johnson, *Lives of the Poets*, vol. 1

p. 155 'justify the ways of God to men': John Leonard (ed.), John Milton, *Paradise Lost*, Book I, line 26 (Penguin Classics, 2002)

p. 155 'God started all the trouble in the first place ... the reason why the poem is so good is that it makes God so bad': William Empson, *Milton's God* (Cambridge University Press, 1961. Revised edition 1981). Quoted in John Leonard (ed.), John Milton, *Paradise Lost*

p. 155 'alleged to have no moral superiority': Zachary Leader, Michael O'Neill (eds.), P. B. Shelley, 'A Defence of Poetry', *The Major Works* (Oxford University Press, 2003)

p. 155 'central Protestant poet': Harold Bloom, *How to Read and Why* (Fourth Estate, 2001)

p. 155 'This day I have begot whom I declare[...]': John Leonard (ed.), John Milton, *Paradise Lost*, Book V, lines 603–8

p. 155 'Him who disobeys': *Paradise Lost*, Book V, lines 611–15

p. 155 'bringing down all mankind rather than one brave but limited general': Harold Bloom, *How to Read and Why*

p. 155–6 'anxiety of influence': Harold Bloom, Margaret Drabble (eds.), *The Oxford Companion to English Literature* (Oxford University Press, 2000)

p. 156 'rhyme being no necessary adjunct or true ornament of poem or good verse': Douglas Bush (ed.), John Milton, *Poetical Works* (Oxford University Press, 1966)

p. 156 'outside the theatre our greatest master of freedom within form': T. S. Eliot, *On Poetry and Poets*

p. 156 'the full beauty of the line is found in its context – and that is conclusive evidence of his supreme mastery': ibid.

p. 156 'secure what came': Arthur Waugh (ed.), Samuel Johnson, *Lives of the Poets*, vol. 1

p. 156 'Milton must be read aloud': Douglas Bush (ed.), John Milton, *Poetical Works*

p. 156 'The mind is its own place, and in itself/Can make a Heav'n of Hell, a Hell of Heav'n . . . Better to reign in Hell, than serve in Heav'n': John Milton, *Paradise Lost*, Book I, lines 224–5, 263

p. 156 'he was a true Poet and of the Devil's party without knowing it': William Blake, Angela Partington (ed.), *The Oxford Dictionary of Quotations* (Oxford University Press, 1992)

p. 156 'all good to me is lost;/Evil, be thou my good': *Paradise Lost*, Book IV, lines 108–9

p. 157 'ye shall not die:/How should ye? by the fruit?/it gives you life/To knowledge': *Paradise Lost*, Book IX, lines 687–8

p. 157 'Adam wedded to another Eve,/Shall I live with her enjoying, I extinct': *Paradise Lost*, Book IX, lines 828–9

p. 157 'flesh of flesh/Bone of my bone thou art, and from thy state/Mine never shall be parted, bliss or woe': *Paradise Lost*, Book IX, lines 914–16

p. 157 'in lust they burn': *Paradise Lost*, Book IX, line 1015

p. 157 'the hast'ning Angel': *Paradise Lost*, Book XII, lines 637

p. 157 'Some natural tears they dropp'd, but wip'd them soon': *Paradise Lost*, Book XII, line 645

p. 157 'The World was all before them': *Paradise Lost*, Book XII, lines 647–9

Christina G. Rossetti, pp. 181–87

p. 181 'Downstairs I laugh, I sport and jest with all;/But in my solitary room above/I turn my face in silence to the wall;/My heart is breaking for a little love': Christina Rossetti, 'L.E.L.', *The Complete Poems* (Penguin Books, 2001)

p. 181 'in the fireless top back bedroom on the corner of the cracked washstand, on the backs of old letters Christina sat writing': C. H. Sisson (ed.), Christina Rossetti, *Selected Poems* (Fyfield Books/ Carcanet, 1984)

p. 181 'shut the door to face the naked truth': Christina Rossetti, 'Memory', *The Complete Poems*

p. 181 'My heart dies inch by inch, the time grows old': Christina Rossetti, 'Monna Innominata', *The Complete Poems*

p. 181 'Nearly every one of her poems was an instance . . . of an emotion': Ford Madox Ford, quoted in C. H. Sisson (ed.), Christina Rossetti, *Selected Poems*

p. 181 'unequalled for its objective expression of happiness denied and a certain unfamiliar steely stoicism': Philip Larkin quoted in C. H. Sisson (ed.), Christina Rossetti, *Selected Poems*

p. 182 'hope deferred': Jan Marsh, *Christina Rossetti: A Literary Biography* (Jonathan Cape, 1994)

p. 182 'I love, as you would have me, God the most; Would not lose Him, but you, must one be lost . . . / This say I, having counted up the cost': C. H. Sisson (ed.), Christina Rossetti, 'Monna Innominata', *Selected Poems*

p. 182 'bringing a case against God': Jan Marsh, *Christina Rossetti: A Literary Biography*

p. 182 'But all night long that voice spake urgently:/"Open to Me/. . .

Rise, let Me in"': Christina Rossetti, 'Despised and Rejected', *The Complete Poems*

p. 182 *'Did I not die for thee?/Do I not live for thee? leave Me tomorrow'*: 'Dost Thou Not Care?', C. H. Sisson (ed.), Christina Rossetti, *Selected Poems*

p. 183 'He broke my will from day to day/He read my yearnings unexpressed/And said them nay . . . But, Christ my God, when will it be/That I may let alone my toil/And rest with Thee?': Christina Rossetti, 'Weary in Well-Doing', *The Complete Poems*

p. 184 'Once upon a time Christina Rossetti was simple': Margaret Reynolds, 'Speaking Unlikenesses' in Mary Arseneau, Antony H. Harrison, Lorraine Janzen Kooistra (eds.), *The Culture of Christina Rossetti: Female Poetics and Victorian Contexts* (Ohio University Press, 1999)

p. 184 'Long ago and long ago': 'Maiden-Song', Christina Rossetti, *The Complete Poems*

The Poems

p. 185 'with a golden curl': Christina Rossetti, 'Goblin Market', *The Complete Poems*

p. 185 'Come buy our orchard fruits,/come buy, come buy': ibid.

p. 185 'sucked and sucked and sucked the more . . . until her lips were sore': ibid.

p. 185 'Kicked and knocked her,/Mauled and mocked her': ibid.

p. 185 'Eat me, drink me, love me;/Laura, make much of me:/For your sake I have braved the glen/and had to do with goblin merchant men': ibid.

p. 185 'there is no friend like a sister/In calm or stormy weather': ibid.

p. 185 'were wives/With children of their own': ibid.

p. 186 'one of the greatest achievements of Victorian poetry': Tom Paulin, *The Second Life of Poems: A Poetry Primer* (Faber and Faber, 2008)

p. 186 'lurked to spy and peer': Christina Rossetti, 'Sister Maude', *The Complete Poems*

p. 186 'But sister Maude, oh sister Maude,/Bide *you* with death and sin': ibid.

p. 186 'Here's friendship for you if you like; but love, – /No, thank you, John': Christina Rossetti, '"No Thank You, John"', *The Complete Poems*

p. 186 'When I am dead, my dearest,/Sing no sad songs for me; . . . I shall not see the shadows,/I shall not feel the rain; . . . Haply I may remember,/And haply may forget': Christina Rossetti, 'Song', *The Complete Poems*

p. 186 'Dost Thou not love me, Lord, or care/For this mine ill?': Christina Rossetti, 'Dost Thou Not Care?', *The Complete Poems*

p. 186 '"Memory" is one of the poems which most merits Larkin's "steely stoicism"': C. H. Sisson (ed.), Christina Rossetti, *Selected Poems*

p. 186 'The first stanza of "Up-Hill" was, as Betty S. Flowers tells us, spoken in a sermon by the then lay-preacher in London, Vincent Van Gogh': Mary Arseneau, Antony H. Harrison, Lorraine Janzen Kooistra (eds.), *The Culture of Christina Rossetti*

Percy Bysshe Shelley, pp. 219–24

p. 219 'I always go on until I am stopped . . . and I am never stopped': Richard Holmes, *Shelley: The Pursuit* (HarperCollins, 1974)

p. 219 'a fountain flowing with the waters of wisdom and delight': P. B. Shelley, 'A Defence of Poetry', *The Major Works* (Oxford World's Classics, 2003)

p. 219 'a sword of lightning, forever unsheathed': ibid.

p. 219 'blew off the lid of his desk': Rupert Christiansen, *Romantic Affinities* (The Bodley Head, 1988)

p. 220 'Every reflecting mind must allow that there is no proof of the existence of a Deity': P. B. Shelley, 'The Necessity of Atheism', *The Major Works*

p. 220 'Love seems inclined to stay in the prison': Ann Wroe, *Being Shelley: The Poet's Search for Himself* (Jonathan Cape, 2007)

p. 220 'They wish to separate us, my beloved; but Death shall unite us': Richard Holmes, *Shelley: The Pursuit*

p. 220 'ten minutes of "happy passion" with Lord Byron': Janet Todd, *Death and the Maidens* (Profile Books, 2007)

p. 221 'I have written fearlessly . . . I believe that Homer, Shakespeare, and Milton wrote with an utter disregard of anonymous censure': Thomas Hutchinson, Humphrey Milford (eds.), Preface to *The Revolt of Islam*, *The Complete Poetical Works* (Oxford University Press, 1917)

p. 221 'Look on my works, ye Mighty, and despair!': 'Ozymandias', Geoffrey Cumberledge (ed.), *Shelley's Poetical Works* (Oxford University Press, 1948)

p. 221 'I change, but I cannot die': P. B. Shelley, 'The Cloud', *The Major Works*

p. 221 'I met Murder on the way–/He had a mask like Castlereagh': *The Mask of Anarchy*, Geoffrey Cumberledge (ed.), *Shelley's Poetical Works*

p. 221 'tameless, and swift, and proud': P. B. Shelley, 'Ode to the West Wind', *The Major Works*

p. 222 'Our sweetest songs are those that tell/of saddest thought': P. B. Shelley, 'To a Skylark', *The Major Works*

p. 222 'the unacknowledged legislators of the world': P. B. Shelley, 'A Defence of Poetry', *The Major Works*

The Poems

p. 223 'The poet and the man are two different natures': P. B. Shelley quoted in Ann Rove, *Being Shelley: The Poet's Search for Himself*

p. 223 'the greatest "High Romantic" of them all': Harold Bloom, *How to Read and Why* (Fourth Estate, 2001)

p. 223 'Even love is sold': *Queen Mab*, Geoffrey Cumberledge (ed.), *Shelley's Poetical Works*

p. 223 'his finest sonnet': Richard Holmes, *Shelley: The Pursuit*

p. 223 'I have lived too long near Lord Byron and the sun has extinguished the glow-worm': Richard Holmes, *Shelley: The Pursuit*

p. 223 'the lady who had left him': 'Julian and Maddalo', Geoffrey Cumberledge (ed.), *Shelley's Poetical Works*

p. 224 'Here lies one whose name was writ in water': Keats's grave, Protestant Cemetery, Rome

p. 224 'And water shall see thee/And fear thee, and fly thee/The waves shall not touch thee/As they pass by thee!': Richard Holmes, *Shelley: The Pursuit*

p. 224 'Then, what is Life?'/Happy those for whom the fold/Of': *The Triumph of Life*, Geoffrey Cumberledge (ed.), *Shelley's Poetical Works*

p. 224 'is how Dante would sound': Harold Bloom, *How to Read and Why*

p. 224 'the most despairing poem, of true eminence, in the language . . . It would bewilder and depress us were it not for its augmented poetic power': ibid.

p. 224 'Nothing of him that doth fade/But doth suffer a sea-change/Into something rich and strange': William Shakespeare, *The Tempest*

INDEX OF FIRST LINES